Best Kept Secrets

of

Peer Code Review

Authors

Jason Cohen

Steven Teleki

Eric Brown

Contributors

Brandon DuRette

Steven Brown

Brandon Fuller

Library of Congress cataloging-in-Publication Data
Cohen, Jason Aaron, 1978-
    Best Kept Secrets of Peer Code Review / Jason Cohen.
    ISBN 1-59916-067-6
    1. Computer software—Quality control. 2. Peer review.

For information on obtaining permission to use material from this work, please submit a written request to:

Smart Bear Inc.
12885 Research Blvd
Suite 209B
Austin, TX 78750
877.501.5651
info@smartbearsoftware.com
http://smartbearsoftware.com

10 9 8 7 6 5 4 3

Table of Contents

Acknowledgements

Thanks to the thousands of users of our software whose feedback has always guided us. Thanks particularly to Eli Abbe, Tom Bentley, Jim Bish, Rolf Campbell, Arthur Castonguay, Dave Curry, Jagdev Dhillon, Brandon Fuller, Terrie Hardie, Chris Holl, Macduff Hughes, Jan Kozlow, Jeff LeJeune, Mark Leyden, Larry Lozares, Hamish Macdonald, Rod Morison, Fabrizio Oddone, Vida Palmer, Carey Parker, Gunnar Piotraszeweski, Roi Sadan, Jacob Schroeder, Andre Stewart, Frank Sueberling, John Theofanopoulos, David Thompson, Dave Tishenkel, Brian Toombs, Thierry Valentin, Alex Vendrow, and Ed Willis. Your tireless and patient efforts continue to shape the future of Smart Bear and peer code review in general.

Thanks to Darla and Leslie Cohen, Sandra Teleki, Roy Paterson, and all the contributors for your diligent editing and great ideas.

Thanks to Beatrice Victoria Rakoff for the original cover art.

This book is especially indebted to Steven Teleki, who not only contributed an entire chapter but also provided inspiration, stories, insight, and wisdom throughout the book.

And a special thank you to Gerry Cullen who continues to show the way.

The Case for Peer Review

The $1 billion bug and why no one talks

about peer code review.

It was only supposed to take an hour.

The bad news was that we had a stack of customer complaints. The latest release had a nasty bug that slipped through QA. The good news was that some of those complaints included descriptions of the problem – an unexpected error dialog box – and one report had an attached log file. We just had to reproduce the problem using the log and add this case to the unit tests. Turn around a quick release from the stable branch and we're golden.

Of course that's not how it turned out. We followed the steps from the log and everything worked fine. QA couldn't reproduce the problem either. Then it turned out the error dialog was a red herring – the real error happened long before the dialog popped up, somewhere deep in the code.

A week later with two developers on the task we finally discovered the cause of the problem. Once we saw the code it was painfully obvious – a certain subroutine didn't check for invalid input. By the time we got the fix out we had twenty more complaints. One potential customer that was trialing the product was never heard from again.

All over a simple bug. Even a cursory glance over the source code would have prevented the wasted time and lost customers.

The worst part is that this isn't an isolated incident. It happens in all development shops. The good news? A policy of peer code review can stop these problems at the earliest stages, before they reach the customer, before it gets expensive.

The case for review: Find bugs early & often

One of our customers set out to test exactly how much money the company would have saved had they used peer review in a certain three-month, 10,000-line project with 10 developers. They tracked how many bugs were found by QA and customers in the subsequent six months. Then they went back and had another group of developers peer-review the code in question. Using metrics from previous releases of this project they knew the average cost of fixing a defect at each phase of development, so they were able to measure directly how much money they would have saved.

The result: Code review would have saved *half* the cost of fixing the bugs. Plus they would have found 162 additional bugs.

Why is the effect of code review so dramatic? A lack of collaboration in the development phase may be the culprit.

With requirements and design you always have meetings. You bring in input from customers, managers, developers, and QA to synthesize a result. You do this because mistakes in requirements or architecture are expensive, possibly leading to lost sales. You debate the relative priorities, difficulty, and long-term merits of your choices.

Saving $150k: A real-world case study

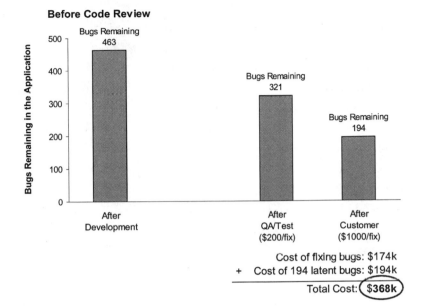

Before Code Review

Cost of fixing bugs: $174k
+   Cost of 194 latent bugs: $194k
—————————————
Total Cost: $368k

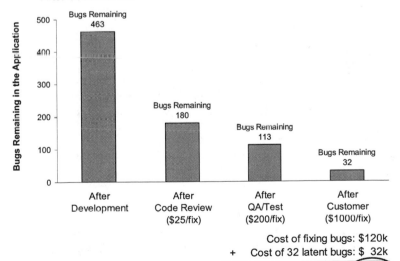

After Code Review

Cost of fixing bugs: $120k
+   Cost of 32 latent bugs: $ 32k
—————————————
Total Cost: $152k

Not so when actually writing the source code. Individual developers type away at the tasks assigned to them. Collaboration is limited to occasional whiteboard drawings and a few shared interfaces. No one is catching the obvious bugs; no one is making sure the documentation matches the code.

Peer code review adds back the collaborative element to this phase of the software development process.

Consider this: Nothing is commercially published without corrections from several professional editors. Find the acknowledgments in any book and you'll find reviewers who helped "remove defects." No matter how smart or diligent the author, the review process is necessary to produce a high-quality work. (And even then, what author hasn't found five more errors after seeing the first edition?)

Why do we think it's any different in software development? Why should we expect our developers to write pages of detailed code (and prose) without mistakes?

We shouldn't. If review works with novels and software design it can also work when writing code. Peer code review adds a much-needed collaborative element to the development phase of the software development process.

The $1 billion bug

In 2005, Adobe attributed $1 billion in revenue to the PDF format[1].

Why is PDF worth $1 billion? Because it's the one format that *everyone* can view and print[2]. It just works. If it loses that

---

[1] Income primarily from the "Adobe Intelligent Documents" division, defined with financial figures in Adobe Systems Incorporated Letter to Stockholders FY 2005.

[2] "At the heart of our enterprise strategy are the free and ubiquitous Adobe Reader software and Adobe Portable Document Format (PDF). Adobe Reader enables users to view, print, and interact with documents across a wide variety of platforms." Ibid, page 6.

status, Adobe loses the edifice built on that format, to which the fiscal year 2005 income statement attributes $1 billion.

Now imagine you are a development manager for Acrobat Reader, Windows Edition. The next major release is due in 9 months and you are responsible for adding five new features. You know how much is riding on Reader and how much revenue – and jobs – depends on its continued success.

So now the question: Which of those five features is so compelling, it would be worth introducing a crash-bug in Reader just to have that feature?

Answer: None!

Nothing is worth losing your position in the industry. But you still must implement new features to keep the technology fresh and competition at bay. So what techniques will you employ in your development process to ensure that no bugs get introduced?

Answer: Everything. Including code review.

Only code review will ensure that this code base – already over ten years old – remains maintainable for the next ten. Only code review will ensure that new hires don't make mistakes that veterans would avoid. And every defect found in code review is another bug that might have gotten through QA and into the hands of a customer.

There are many organizations in this position: The cost of losing market position is unthinkably large, so the cost of every defect is similarly large. In fact, any software company with a mature product offering is almost certainly in this position.

This doesn't mean they implement code review no matter what the costs; developer time is still an expensive commodity. It does mean that they're taking the time to understand this process which, if implemented properly, is a proven method for significantly reducing the number of delivered bugs, keeping code maintainable, and getting new hires productive quickly and safely.

But you don't need to have $1 billion at stake to be interested in code quality and maintainability. Delivering bugs to QA costs money; delivering bugs to customers costs a lot of money and loss of goodwill.

But if code review works this well, why don't more people talk about it? Is anyone really doing it?

Why code review is a secret

In 1991, OOP was the Next Big Thing. But strangely, at OOPSLA there were precious few papers, light on content, and yet the attendees admitted to each other in hallway talk that their companies were fervently using the new techniques and gaining significant improvements in code reusability and in breaking down complex systems.

So why weren't they talking publicly? Because the development groups that truly understood the techniques of OOP had a competitive advantage. OOP was new and everyone was learning empirically what worked and what didn't; why give up that hard-earned knowledge to your competitors?

A successfully-implemented code review process is a competitive advantage. No one wants to give away the secret of how to release fewer defects efficiently.

When we got started no one was talking about code review in the press, so we didn't think many people were doing it. But our experience has made it clear that peer code review is widespread at companies who are serious about code quality.

But the techniques are still a secret![3] Peer code review has the potential to take too much time to be worth the gain in bug-fixing, code maintainability, or in mentoring new developers. The

---

[3] Some companies have published case studies on effectiveness of heavyweight inspection processes. In our experience, the overwhelming majority of code review processes are not heavyweight, and those studies are often statistically-insignificant. Details on this and our own case study are given in several other essays in this collection.

techniques that provide the benefits of peer code review while mitigating the pitfalls and managing developers' time are competitive advantages that no one wants to reveal.

Unfortunately for these successful software development organizations, we make a living making code review accessible and efficient for everyone. And that's what this book is about.

I'm interested. What next?

So code review works, but what if developers waste too much time doing it? What if the social ramifications of personal critiquing ruin morale? How can review be implemented in a measurable way so you can identify process problems?

We cover case studies of review in the real world and show which conclusions you can draw from them (and which you can't). We give our own case study of 2500 reviews. We give pro's and con's for the five most common types of review. We explain how to take advantage of the positive social and personal aspects of review as well as ways managers can mitigate negative emotions that can arise. We explain how to implement a review within a CMMI/PSP/TSP context. We give specific advice on how to construct a peer review process that meets specific goals. Finally, we describe a tool that our customers have used to make certain kinds of reviews as painless and efficient as possible.

Code review can be practical, efficient, and even fun.

Resistance to Code Review

Why some developers resist code review and how new tools change the game.

Written by Eric Brown.

"Code review." Say this in a room of programmers and you'll feel a sudden deceleration, as if a little life force were suddenly sucked out of everyone. As a programmer, you have little tolerance for anything that impedes your productivity. True programmers have a sense of streaming creativity as they write code to solve problems or create innovations. This stream has a continuity that ebbs as you have to pause to answer the phone or talk with the colleague who just walked into your office, and flows after you have solved a particularly difficult obstacle or feel the surge of caffeine from the coffee you just finished. But call a department meeting or schedule a code review, and the flow stops outright. The prospect of having to sit and listen to others talk about customer requirements, or new quality measures, or discuss whether there are enough comments in the code for the code-challenged guy down the hall to understand what he's supposed to do, makes any programmer squirm.

The idea of code review has been around almost as long as programming itself. This isn't surprising, as most of us figure out in elementary school the value of double-checking our work. Authors have editors, accountants have auditors, and scientists have peer review journals. Disciplines of every shape and form have their own self-check, collaborative processes, whether formal or informal. Software developers, too, know the value of bouncing ideas and work off their peers. And in circumstances where getting the code right is especially important, developers instinctively turn to another set of eyes to double-check their work.

Design documentation is traditionally the first (and often only) place when peer review occurs in software development organizations. The importance of getting the conceptual design right is widely recognized and practiced. However, it's now also widely recognized that the static, non-iterative design-then-implementation model of software development, known as the waterfall model, isn't effective at producing quality products on a competitive schedule. Software today is usually developed in an agile and iterative process, often with customer input and changing requirements feeding back into the product content during development. But iterative development means rapidly-changing code, which in turn creates continuous opportunities where peer review would be conducive to and perhaps even necessary for software quality.

Another point where peer review has an obvious place is in changes to a released code base. The impact of modifying code that already exists on installed systems is much greater than code that has yet to be released to customers. And there are many situations where the impact of changing released code can be orders of magnitude more important and costly, such as mission-critical processes, embedded systems, or industry-standard applications with massive install bases.

In today's software development environments, regular peer review should be a logical component of the development process. Few developers and software project managers would argue that these are direct benefits of conducting code reviews:

- Improved code quality
- Fewer defects in code
- Improved communication about code content
- Education of junior programmers

And these indirect benefits are byproducts of code review:

- Shorter development/test cycles
- Reduced impact on technical support
- More customer satisfaction
- More maintainable code

And yet, some development groups still don't use code review as a regular part of their process are. Why is this? There are two primary, straightforward reasons:

1. Programmer egos
2. The hassle of packaging source code for review and scheduling review meetings

Let's talk about egos first. When someone else is looking over their work, any programmer will naturally evaluate what the person thinks of it. This can either be interpreted as a constructive process or a critical one, and this interpretation can create 2 different classes of programmers. The first class are collaborators – programmers who, when they are confronted with a problem, will do what it takes to figure it out (or at least come up with a workaround), which often includes asking a peer who knows the answer already or is willing to bounce around ideas. They see and use peer review as a beneficial process. The second class are isolationists – those programmers who, when confronted with a problem they are unable to solve, will continue to thrash unproductively on it rather than reveal to their peers that they need help. On a side note, this dichotomy of approaches certainly isn't unique to programmers, and exists on a larger scale in personalities in general.

Why do these classes tend to be so distinct among programmers? The main reason is the latter class of programmer tends to have a short career in software development. Their body of knowledge becomes constrained to what they can figure out on their own, which even for the brightest individuals (in a field of bright individuals) is limited.

In 2002 it was reported that the average career in high-tech lasts 8 years. That's too long to waste getting yourself straightened out. Attitude can be as important as aptitude. A programmer needs the ability to work in teams, to listen carefully, to take risks, and to learn from their mistakes, in order to survive in the typically fast-paced environments in high-tech fields. A continuous interest in learning consistently enhances and sharpens skills, and allows programmers to continue to be productive (and marketable!) in a constantly changing field.

Many developers already understand the value of collaborative work. Why, then, are code reviews still uncommon with many developers? If you're a programmer, you probably intuitively know the answer. And if not, to understand the answer you should know first how programmers work.

Programming is an art and a discipline. A programmer tends to have to create solutions, as opposed to engineering fields where most problems are categorized and the known solutions applied.

A programmer creates/invents a solution that is both sufficient and necessary. A programmer works in bursts of an altered and heightened state of consciousness to produce. If you ask someone who works in this mode to provide a weekly status report, or attend a corporate pep rally, or sit through the weekly department meeting, you'll typically be met with a groan of disdain, or an excuse about having that Sev-3 deferred feature they've been meaning to get to.

When I worked as a device driver developer for a large software and hardware corporation, our first-line manager was highly non-technical. He always had the same insight into any bug we were trying to isolate: "You should just set a flag." Most programmers have a primal fear of having to explain something to, or suffer pointless questions from, someone like this. So when you ask a programmer to extract the last few revisions of someone else's code from source control, print them out and highlight the changes, and then bring them to a meeting for discussion with other people, including someone like my old manager, you will sense that life force being sucked away.

We programmers intuitively evaluate cost-benefit decisions. We decide when to use an iterative search or implement our own quicksort routine, or when to use source code available in the public domain versus writing our own component from scratch, or when a release has sufficiently few and minor defects that it is ready to ship. The reason some programmers are still reluctant to do code reviews is an intuitive decision that the cost-benefit of doing a review – in terms of improved code quality weighed against the pain and time conducting it takes – just isn't worth it.

But code review doesn't have to be painful anymore. The process of code review, like the software industry itself, has changed dramatically over the last 10 or 20 years. Just as modern IDE's eliminate the labor and risk of refactoring, there are now software tools for peer code review that solve these issues of collaboration and source control system integration.

It has also been shown that, when done properly, fast light-weight code review can be just as effective as traditional meetings-based inspections. Tools designed for this purpose cut out drudgery and give managers their reports without burdening the developer.

There's no longer an excuse for not reviewing code.

Five Types of Review

Pros and cons of formal, over-the-shoulder, e-mail pass-around, pair-programming, and tool-assisted reviews.

There are many ways to skin a cat. I can think of four right off the bat. There are also many ways to perform a peer review, each with pros and cons.

Formal inspections

For historical reasons, "formal" reviews are usually called "inspections." This is a hold-over from Michael Fagan's seminal 1976 study at IBM regarding the efficacy of peer reviews. He tried many combinations of variables and came up with a procedure for reviewing up to 250 lines of prose or source code. After 800 iterations he came up with a formalized inspection strategy and to this day you can pay him to tell you about it (company name: Fagan Associates). His methods were further studied and expanded upon by others, most notably Tom Gilb and Karl Wiegers.

In general, a "formal" review refers to a heavy-process review with three to six participants meeting together in one room with print-outs and/or a projector. Someone is the "moderator" or "controller" and acts as the organizer, keeps everyone on task, controls the pace of the review, and acts as arbiter of disputes. Everyone reads through the materials beforehand to properly prepare for the meeting.

Each participant will be assigned a specific "role." A "reviewer" might be tasked with critical analysis while an "observer" might be called in for domain-specific advice or to learn how to do reviews properly. In a Fagan Inspection, a "reader" looks at source code only for comprehension – not for critique – and presents this to the group. This separates what the author intended from what is actually presented; often the author himself is able to pick out defects given this third-party description.

When defects are discovered in a formal review, they are usually recorded in great detail. Besides the general location of the error in the code, they include details such as severity (e.g. major, minor), type (e.g. algorithm, documentation, data-usage, error-handling), and phase-injection (e.g. developer error, design oversight, requirements mistake). Typically this information is kept in a database so defect metrics can be analyzed from many angles and possibly compared to similar metrics from QA.

Formal inspections also typically record other metrics such as individual time spent during pre-meeting reading and during the meeting itself, lines-of-code inspection rates, and problems encountered with the process itself. These numbers and comments are examined periodically in process-improvement meetings; Fagan Inspections go one step further and requires a process-rating questionnaire after each meeting to help with the improvement step.

A Typical Formal Inspection Process

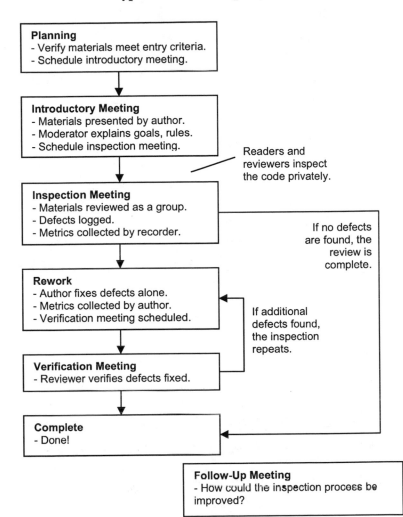

Figure 1: Typical workflow for a "formal" inspection. Not shown are the artifacts created by the review: The defect log, meeting notes, and metrics log. Some inspections also have a closing questionnaire used in the follow-up meeting.

Formal inspections' greatest asset is also its biggest drawback: When you have many people spending lots of time reading code and discussing its consequences, you are going to identify a lot of defects. And there are plenty of studies that show formal inspections can identify a large number of problems in source code.

But most organizations cannot afford to tie up that many people for that long. You also have to schedule the meetings – a daunting task in itself and one that ends up consuming extra developer time[1]. Finally, most formal methods require training to be effective, and this is an additional time and expense that is difficult to accept, especially when you aren't already used to doing code reviews.

Many studies in the past 15 years have come out demonstrating that other forms of review uncover just as many defects as do formal reviews but with much less time and training[2]. This result – anticipated by those who have tried many types of review – has put formal inspections out of favor in the industry.

After all, if you can get all the proven benefits of formal inspections but occupy 1/3 the developer time, that's clearly better.

So let's investigate some of these other techniques.

Over-the-shoulder reviews

This is the most common and informal of code reviews. An "over-the-shoulder" review is just that – a developer standing over the author's workstation while the author walks the reviewer through a set of code changes.

Typically the author "drives" the review by sitting at the keyboard and mouse, opening various files, pointing out the changes and explaining why it was done this way. The author can present the changes using various tools and even run back and forth between changes and other files in the project. If the reviewer sees

---

[1] See the Votta 1993 case study detailed elsewhere in this collection.
[2] See the case study survey elsewhere in this collection for details.

something amiss, they can engage in a little "spot pair-programming" as the author writes the fix while the reviewer hovers. Bigger changes where the reviewer doesn't need to be involved are taken off-line.

With modern desktop-sharing software a so-called "over-the-shoulder" review can be made to work over long distances. This complicates the process because you need schedule these sharing meetings and communicate over the phone. Standing over a shoulder allows people to point, write examples, or even go to a whiteboard for discussion; this is more difficult over the Internet.

The most obvious advantage of over-the-shoulder reviews is simplicity in execution. Anyone can do it, any time, without training. It can also be deployed whenever you need it most – an especially complicated change or an alteration to a "stable" code branch.

As with all in-person reviews, over-the-shoulders lend them-selves to learning and sharing between developers and gets people to interact in person instead of hiding behind impersonal email and instant-messages. You naturally talk more when you can blurt out and idea rather than making some formal "defect" in a database somewhere.

Unfortunately, the informality and simplicity of the process also leads to a mountain of shortcomings. First, this is not an enforceable process – there's nothing that lets a manager know whether all code changes are being reviewed. In fact, there are no metrics, reports, or tools that measure anything at all about the process.

Second, it's easy for the author to unintentionally miss a change. Countless times we've observed a review that completes, the author checks in his changes, and when he sees the list of files just checked in he says "Oh, did I change that one?" Too late!

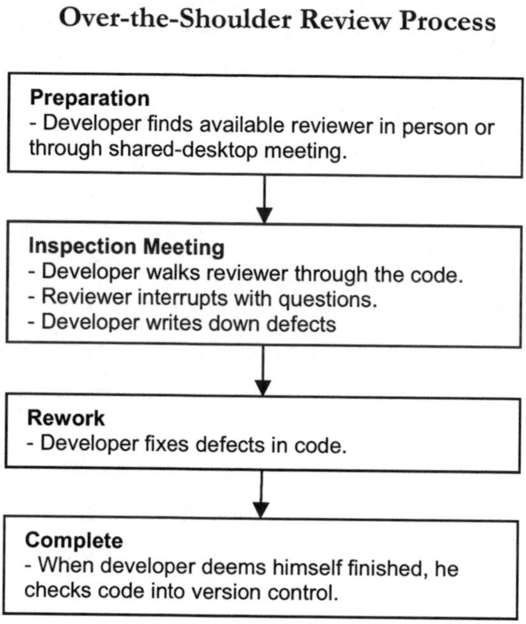

Over-the-Shoulder Review Process

Preparation
- Developer finds available reviewer in person or through shared-desktop meeting.

Inspection Meeting
- Developer walks reviewer through the code.
- Reviewer interrupts with questions.
- Developer writes down defects

Rework
- Developer fixes defects in code.

Complete
- When developer deems himself finished, he checks code into version control.

Figure 2: A typical Over-the-shoulder code walk-through process. Typically no review artifacts are created.

Third, when a reviewer reports defects and leaves the room, rarely does the reviewer return to verify that the defects were fixed properly and that no new defects were introduced. If you're not verifying that defects are fixed, the value of finding them is diminished.

There is another effect of over-the-shoulder reviews which some people consider to be an advantage but others a drawback.

Because the author is controlling the pace of the review, often the reviewer is led too hastily through the code. The reviewer might not ponder over a complex portion of code. The reviewer doesn't get a chance to poke around in other source files to confirm that a change won't break something else. The author might explain something that clarifies the code to the reviewer, but the next developer who reads that code won't have the advantage of that explanation unless it is encoded as a comment in the code. It's difficult for a reviewer to be objective and aware of these issues while being driven through the code with an expectant developer peering up at him.

For example, say the author was tasked with fixing a bug where a portion of a dialog was being drawn incorrectly. After wrestling with the Windows GUI documentation, he finally discovers an undocumented "feature" in the draw-text API call that was causing the problems. He works around the bug with some new code and fixes the problem. When the reviewer gets to this work-around, it looks funny at first.

"Why did you do this," asks the reviewer, "the Windows GUI API will do this for you."

"Yeah, I thought so too," responds the author, "but it turns out it doesn't actually handle this case correctly. So I had to call it a different way in this case."

It's all too easy for the reviewer to accept the changes. But the next developer that reads this code will have the same question, and might even remove the work-around in an attempt to make the code cleaner. "After all," says the next developer, "the Windows API does this for us, so no need for this extra code!"

On the other hand, not all prompting is bad. With changes that touch many files it's often useful to review the files in a particular order. And sometimes a change will make sense to a future reader, but the reviewer might need an explanation for why things were changed from the way they were.

Finally, over-the-shoulder reviews by definition don't work when the author and reviewer aren't in the same building; they probably should also be in nearby offices. For any kind of remote review, you need to invoke some electronic communication. Even with desktop-sharing and speakerphones, many of the benefits of face-to-face interactions are lost.

E-mail pass-around reviews

This is the second-most common form of informal code review, and the technique preferred by most open-source projects. Here, whole files or changes are packaged up by the author and sent to reviewers via e-mail. Reviewers examine the files, ask questions and discuss with the author and other developers, and suggest changes.

The hardest part of the e-mail pass-around is in finding and collecting the files under review. On the author's end, he has to figure out how to gather the files together. For example, if this is a review of changes being proposed to check into version control, the user has to identify all the files added, deleted, and modified, copy them somewhere, then download the previous versions of those files (so reviewers can see what was changed), and organize the files so the reviewers know which files should be compared with which others. On the reviewing end, reviewers have to extract those files from the e-mail and generate differences between each.

The version control system can be of some assistance. Typically that system can report on which files have been altered and can be made to extract previous versions. Although some people write their own scripts to collect all these files, most use commercial tools that do the same thing and can handle the myriad of corner-cases arising from files in various states and client/server configurations.

The version control system can also assist by sending the e-mails out automatically. For example, a version control server-side "check-in" trigger can send e-mails depending on who checked in the code (e.g. the lead developer of each group reviews code from members of that group) and which files were changed (e.g. some files are "owned" by a user who is best-qualified to review the changes). The automation is helpful, but for many code review processes you want to require reviews before check-in, not after.

E-Mail Pass-Around Process: Post Check-In Review

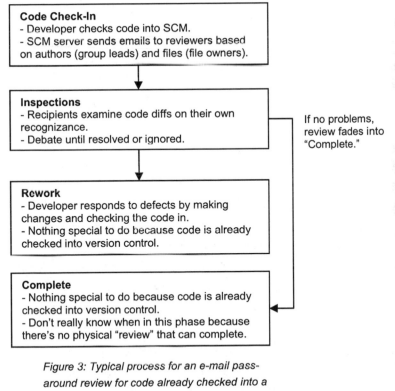

Figure 3: Typical process for an e-mail pass-around review for code already checked into a version control system. These phases are not this distinct in reality because there's no tangible "review" object.

Like over-the-shoulder reviews, e-mail pass-arounds are easy to implement, although more time-consuming because of the file-gathering. But unlike over-the-shoulder reviews, they work equally well with developers working across the hall or across an ocean. And you eliminate the problem of the authors coaching the reviewers through the changes.

Another unique advantage of e-mail pass-arounds is the ease in which other people can be brought into the review. Perhaps there is a domain expert for a section of code that a reviewer wants to get an opinion from. Perhaps the reviewer wants to defer to another reviewer. Or perhaps the e-mail is sent to many people at once, and those people decide for themselves who are best qualified to review which parts of the code. This inclusiveness is difficult with in-person reviews and with formal inspections where all participants need to be invited to the meeting in advance.

Yet another advantage of e-mail pass-arounds is they don't knock reviewers out of "the zone." It's well established that it takes a developer 15 minutes to get into "the zone" where they are immersed in their work and are highly productive[3]. Even just asking a developer for a review knocks him out of the zone – even if the response is "I'm too busy." With e-mails, reviewers can work during a self-prescribed break so they can stay in the zone for hours at a time.

There are several important drawbacks to the e-mail pass-around review method. The biggest is that for all but the most trivial reviews, it can rapidly become difficult to track the various threads of conversation and code changes. With several discussions concerning a few different areas of the code, possibly inviting other developers to the fray, it's hard to track what everyone's saying or whether the group is getting to a consensus.

---

[3] For a fun read on this topic, see "Where do These People Get Their (Unoriginal) Ideas?" Joel On Software. Joel Spolsky, Apr 29, 2000.

E-Mail Pass-Around Process: Pre Check-In Review

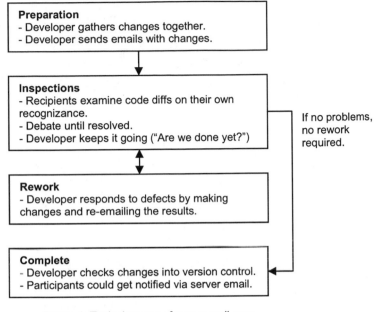

Figure 4: *Typical process for an e-mail pass-around review for code already checked into a version control system. These phases are not this distinct in reality because there's no tangible "review" object.*

This is even more prominent with over-seas reviews; ironic since one of the distinct advantages of e-mail pass-arounds is that they can be done with remote developers. An over-seas review might take many days as each "back and forth" can take a day, so it might take five days to complete a review instead of thirty minutes. This means many simultaneous reviews, and that means even more difficulties keeping straight the conversations and associated code changes.

Imagine a developer in Hyderabad opening Outlook to discover 25 emails from different people discussing aspects of three different code changes he's made over the last few days. It will take a while just to dig though that before any real work can begin.

For all their advantages over over-the-shoulder reviews, e-mail pass-arounds share some disadvantages. Product managers are still not sure whether all code changes are being reviewed. Even with version control server-side triggers, all you know is that changes were sent out – not that anyone actually looked at them. And if there was a consensus that certain defects needed to be fixed, you cannot verify that those fixes were made properly. Also there are still no metrics to measure the process, determine efficiency, or measure the effect of a change in the process.

With e-mail pass-arounds we've seen that with the introduction of a few tools (i.e. e-mail, version control client-side scripts for file-collection and server-side scripts for workflow automation) we were able to gain several benefits over over-the-shoulder reviews without introducing significant drawbacks. Perhaps by the introduction of more sophisticated, specialized tools we can continue to add benefits while removing the remaining drawbacks.

Tool-Assisted reviews

This refers to any process where specialized tools are used in all aspects of the review: collecting files, transmitting and displaying files, commentary and defects among all participants, collecting metrics, and giving product managers and administrators some control over the workflow.

There are several key elements that must be present in a review tool if it is going to solve the major problems with other types of review[4]:

---

[4] In the interest of full-disclosure, Smart Bear Software, the company that employs the author of this essay, sells a popular peer code review tool called Code Collaborator for exactly this purpose. This product is described in a

Automated File Gathering

As we discussed in the e-mail pass-around section, you can't have developers spending time manually gathering files and differences for review. A tool must integrate with your version control system to extract current and previous versions so reviewers can easily see the changes under review.

Ideally the tool can do this both with local changes not yet checked into version control and with already-checked-in changes (e.g. by date, label, branch, or unique change-list number). Even if you're not doing both types of review today, you'll want the option in the future.

Combined Display: Differences, Comments, Defects

One of the biggest time-sinks with any type of review is in reviewers and developers having to associate each sub-conversation with a particular file and line number. The tool must be able to display files and before/after file differences in such a manner that conversations are threaded and no one has to spend time cross-referencing comments, defects, and source code.

Automated Metrics Collection

On one hand, accurate metrics are the only way to understand your process and the only way to measure the changes that occur when you change the process. On the other hand, no developer wants to review code while holding a stopwatch and wielding line-counting tools.

A tool that automates collection of key metrics is the only way to keep developers happy (i.e. no extra work for them) and get meaningful metrics on your process. A full discussion of review metrics and what they mean appears in another essay, but your tool should at least collect these three rates: kLOC/hour (inspection

---

different essay in this collection; this section will discuss general ways in which tools can assist the review process.

rate), defects/hour (defect rate), and defects/kLOC (defect density).

Review Enforcement

Almost all other types of review suffer from the problem of product managers not knowing whether developers are reviewing all code changes or whether reviewers are verifying that defects are indeed fixed and didn't cause new defects. A tool should be able to enforce this workflow at least at a reporting level (for passive workflow enforcement) and at best at the version control level (with server-side triggers that enforce workflow at the version control level).

Clients and Integrations

Some developers like command-line tools. Others prefer integrations with IDE's and version control GUI clients. Administrators like zero-installation web clients. It's important that a tool supports many ways to read and write data in the system.

Developer tools also have a habit of needing to be integrated with other tools. Version control clients are inside IDE's. Issue-trackers are correlated with version control changes. Similarly, your review tool needs to integrate with your other tools – everything from IDE's and version control clients to metrics and reports. A bonus is a tool that exposes a public API so you can make customizations and detailed integrations yourself.

If your tool satisfies this list of requirements, you'll have the benefits of e-mail pass-around reviews (works with multiple, possibly-remote developers, minimizes interruptions) but without the problems of no workflow enforcement, no metrics, and wasting time with file/difference packaging, delivery, and inspection.

The drawback of any tool-assisted review is cost – either in cash for a commercial tool or as time if developed in-house. You also need to make sure the tool is flexible enough to handle your specific code review process; otherwise you might find the tool driving your process instead of vice-versa.

Although tool-assisted reviews can solve the problems that plague typical code reviews, there is still one other technique that, while not often used, has the potential to find even more defects than standard code review.

Pair-Programming

Most people associate pair-programming with XP[5] and agile development in general, but it's also a development process that incorporates continuous code review. Pair-programming is two developers writing code at a single workstation with only one developer typing at a time and continuous free-form discussion and review.

Studies of pair-programming have shown it to be very effective at both finding bugs and promoting knowledge transfer. And some developers really enjoy doing it.

There's a controversial issue about whether pair-programming reviews are better, worse, or complementary to more standard reviews. The reviewing developer is deeply involved in the code, giving great thought to the issues and consequences arising from different implementations. On the one hand this gives the reviewer lots of inspection time and a deep insight into the problem at hand, so perhaps this means the review is more effective. On the other hand, this closeness is exactly what you don't want in a reviewer; just as no author can see all typos in his own writing, a reviewer too close to the code cannot step back and critique it from a fresh and unbiased position. Some people suggest using both techniques – pair-programming for the deep review and a follow-up standard review for fresh eyes. Although

---

5 Extreme Programming is perhaps the most talked-about form of agile development. Learn more at http://www.extremeprogramming.org.

this takes a lot of developer time to implement, it would seem that this technique would find the greatest number of defects. We've never seen anyone do this in practice.

The single biggest complaint about pair-programming is that it takes too much time. Rather than having a reviewer spend 15-30 minutes reviewing a change that took one developer a few days to make, in pair-programming you have two developers on the task the entire time.

Some developers just don't like pair-programming; it depends on the disposition of the developers and who is partnered with whom. Pair-programming also does not address the issue of remote developers.

A full discussion of the pros and cons of pair-programming in general is beyond our scope.

Conclusion

Each of the five types of review is useful in its own way. Formal inspections and pair-programming are proven techniques but require large amounts of developer time and don't work with remote developers. Over-the-shoulder reviews are easiest to implement but can't be implemented as a controlled process. E-mail pass-around and tool-assisted reviews strike a balance between time invested and ease of implementation.

And any kind of code review is better than nothing.

Brand New Information

What modern literature has to say about code

review; what studies do and don't agree on.

An Amazon search for books on "code inspection" turns up only one item[1]: The 1974, out-of-print, 29-page article by Michael Fagan of IBM. In that year, IBM sold the model 3330-11 disk drive for $111,600. A megabyte of RAM would set you back $75,000. The PDP-11 was still the best-selling minicomputer.

Everything has changed since then: programming languages, development techniques, application complexity and organization, levels of abstraction, and even the type of person who decides to enter the field.

But there hasn't been much change to the accepted wisdom of how to conduct proper code inspections. Some of Fagan's ideas are as applicable as ever, but surely there must be something

---

[1] Ignoring two "technical articles" and books on home and construction inspections.

new. Inspecting assembly code in OS/360 is nothing like running down the implications of a code change in an object-oriented interpreted language running in a 3-tier environment. Calling inspection meetings with 5 participants doesn't work in the world of remote-site development and agile methodologies.

This essay is a survey of relatively recent studies on peer review and inspection techniques. We point out results common to all studies and results that vary widely between studies.

There is an emphasis here on the timeliness of the study. You won't see the seminal works of Fagan, Gilb, and Wiegers[2]. Some of the original ideas are still as applicable as ever, but of course some things have changed. We don't want to parrot the accepted wisdom of the great men who started the theory of code reviews, but instead to survey what appears to be the state of affairs in the modern world of software development.

Votta 1993[3], Conradi 2003[4], Kelly 2003[5]: Are review meetings necessary?

One of the most controversial questions in code review is: Does every inspection need a meeting? Michael Fagan, the father of code inspection, has insisted since 1976 that the inspection

---

[2] Nothing here should be construed as a slight against the excellent work, tradition, and success established by these men. The author of this essay highly recommends Wieger's 2002 *Peer Reviews in Software* as the most readable, practical guide to formal reviews.

[3] Lawrence G. Votta, Jr., Does every inspection need a meeting?, *Proceedings of the 1st ACM SIGSOFT symposium on Foundations of software engineering*, p.107-114, December 08-10, 1993, Los Angeles, California, United States

[4] Reidar Conradi, Parastoo Mohagheghi, Tayyaba Arif, Lars Christian Hegde, Geir Arne Bunde, and Anders Pedersen; Object-Oriented Reading Techniques for Inspection of UML Models – An Industrial Experiment. In *European Conference on Object-Oriented Programming* ECOOP'03. Springer-Verlag, Darmstadt, Germany, pages 483-501

[5] Kelly, D. and Shepard, T. 2003. An experiment to investigate interacting versus nominal groups in software inspection. In *Proceedings of the 2003 Conference of the Centre For Advanced Studies on Collaborative Research* (Toronto, Ontario, Canada, October 06 - 09, 2003). IBM Centre for Advanced Studies Conference. IBM Press, 122-134.

meeting is where defects are primarily detected, but research in intervening thirty years has not been so strongly conclusive.

The first, most famous attack on the value traditionally associated with meetings came from Lawrence Votta from AT&T Bell Labs in 1993. He identified the five reasons most cited by both managers and software developers in support of inspection meetings:

1. Synergy. Teams find faults that no individual reviewer would be able to find.
2. Education. Less experienced developers and reviewers learn from their more experienced peers.
3. Deadline. Meetings create a schedule that people must work towards.
4. Competition. Ego leads to personal incentive to contribute and improve.
5. Process. Inspections simply require meetings. That's the official process.

However, in his 1993 seminal paper based on his own research and that of others, Votta argued that:

1. Synergy. Meetings tend to identify false-positives rather than find new defects. (More below.)
2. Education. Education by observation is usually unsuccessful; some researchers condemn it completely.
3. Deadlines. Process deadlines are important but could be enforced without meetings per se, or at least without heavy-weight meetings.
4. Competition. Competition is still achieved with any peer review. Some competition destroys teamwork, e.g. between designers and testers.
5. Process. Process is important but facts, not "tradition," should be used to determine the process.

Furthermore, although Votta agreed with the prevailing claims that code inspections save time by detecting defects early in the development process, he pointed out that the founders of inspection did not properly consider the amount of time consumed by the inspection meeting. For example, one study of formal inspection showed that 20% of the requirements and design phase was spent just waiting for a review to start! The time spent in preparing, scheduling, and waiting for reviews is significant and grows with the number of meeting participants, yet this time is ignored in the usual cost-benefit analysis.

Recall that "meeting synergy" was cited most often by both developers and managers as well as by the literature as the primary advantage of inspection meetings. Here "synergy" refers to the team effect that a group of people performs better than any of its members; in particular, that a group-inspection will necessarily uncover more defects than the reviewers individually.

Votta set out to test this hypothesis by measuring the percentage of defects found in inspection meetings as opposed to the private code readings that precede those meetings. His findings are summarized in Figure 5.

As it turned out, meetings contributed only 4% of the defects found in the inspections as a whole. Statistically larger than zero, but Votta asks "Is the benefit of ~4% increase in faults found at the collection meeting (for whatever reason) worth the cost of $T_{collection}$ [wasted time[6]] and the reviewer's extra time? The answer is no."

Strong words! But surely there are other benefits to inspection meetings besides just uncovering defects?

---

[6] Votta identifies three components to wasted time: (1) hazard cost of being later to market, (2) carrying cost of development when developers are in meetings instead of writing code, and (3) rework cost when authors continue to develop the work product only to have the work later invalidated by faults found in inspection.

Defects Found By Inspection Phase

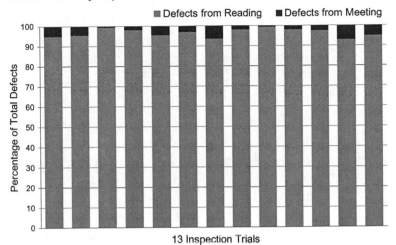

Figure 5: Votta's results demonstrating that inspection meetings contribute only an additional
4% to the number of defects already found by private code-readings.

In 2003, Diane Kelly and Terry Shepard at the Royal Military
College of Canada set up an experiment comparing reviewers in
isolation versus group meetings. Would the results support or
contradict Votta? And besides the quantity of defects, would there
be a difference in other important factors such as the rate at which
defects were uncovered or a reduction in false-positives that waste
authors' time?

In Kelly's case, groups of developers read code individually to
detect as many defects as possible. Then each group got together
in an inspection meeting. If proponents of traditional inspections
are correct, significant numbers of defects will be found during the
meeting phase, especially compared with the reading phase. If

Votta's conclusions are correct, we should expect to see few defects detected in the meeting but some thrown out during the meeting (i.e. removal of false-positives or confusing points in the code).

In total, 147 defects were found during the reading phases[7]. Of these, 39 (26%) were discarded during meetings. Although some of these were due to false-positives (i.e. the reviewer was incorrect in believing there was a defect), in most cases poor documentation or style in the code lead the reviewer to believe there was a problem. Kelly suggests that these should probably be considered "defects" after all.

So the meeting did throw out false-positives – a useful thing – but what about uncovering new defects? Votta would guess that very few new defects would be found. With Kelly the meeting phases added only 20 new defects to the existing 147. Furthermore, of those 20, two-thirds were relatively trivial in nature. So not only did the meeting phases not contribute significantly to overall defect counts, the contribution was generally of a surface-level nature rather than logic-level or algorithmic-level.

Perhaps we should not be surprised by all this. Detecting problems in algorithms generally requires concentration and thought – a single-minded activity that isn't encouraged in the social milieu of a meeting. Are you more likely to discover the bug in a binary-search algorithm by debate or by tracing through code-paths by yourself?

Besides the quantity of defects, it is also useful to consider how much time was consumed by each of these phases. After all, if the review meeting is very fast, the elimination of the false-positives would make it worthwhile even if no additional defects are found.

---

[7] Developers inspecting code in isolation will find duplicate defects; we probably don't want to count these in the analysis. The researchers found only 10 of the 147 were duplicates.

Kelly found that about two-thirds of total person-hours were spent in reading and one-third in meetings. This leads to a defect discovery rate of 1.7 defects per hour for reading and 1.2 for meeting. Reading is 50% more efficient in finding defects than are meetings.

Yet another direct test of Votta's contentions came from a different angle in 2003 from a joint effort conducted by Reidar Conradi between Ericsson Norway and two Norwegian colleges, NTNU and Agder University. The goal of the experiments was to measure the impact of certain reading techniques for UML model inspections. Votta experimented with design reviews, Kelly with source code, and now Conradi would examine architecture reviews.

The stated goal of the study was to determine the effectiveness of "tailored Object-Oriented Reading Techniques" on UML inspections. They collected separate data on defect detection during the reading phase and the meeting phase. Their purpose was not to support or invalidate Votta's results, but their data can be applied to that purpose. Indeed, in their own paper they causally mention that their data just happens to be perfectly in line with Votta's.

In particular, in 38 experimentally-controlled inspections they found that 25% of the time was spent reading, 75% of the time in meetings, and yet 80% of the defects were found during reading! They were 12 times more efficient at finding defects by reading than by meeting. Furthermore, in their case they had 5-7 people in each meeting – several more than Kelly or Votta or even Fagan recommends – so the number of defects found per man-hour was vanishingly small.

Other research confirms these results[8]. Because the reduction of false-positives appears to be the primary effect of the inspection

---

[8] For example, see L. Land, C. Sauer and R. Jeffery's convincing 1997 experiment testing the role of meetings with regard to finding additional defects and

meeting, many researchers conclude that a short meeting with two participants – maybe even by e-mail instead of face-to-face – should be sufficient to get the benefits of the meeting without the drawbacks. The value of detecting false-positives in the first place is questioned because often these are a result of poorly-written code and so often shouldn't be discarded anyway. Given all this, some even suggest that the extra engineering time taken up by implementing fixes for so-called false-positive defects is still less than the time it takes to identify the defects as false, and therefore we should dispense with meetings all together!

Blakely 1991: Hewlett Packard[9]

Hewlett Packard has a long history of code inspections. In 1988 a company-wide edict required a 10x code quality improvement – a tall order for any development organization, but at least it was a measurable goal. They turned to design and code inspections as part of their effort to achieve this, and management sanctioned a pilot program implemented by a development group in the Application Support Division.

Their conclusion: "Based on the data collected about the use of code inspections, and the data concerning the cost of finding and repairing defects after the product has been released to the customer, it is clear that the implementation of code inspections as a regular part of the development cycle is beneficial compared to the costs associated with fixing defects found by customers."

---

removing false-positives. Validating the defect detection performance advantage of group designs for software reviews: report of a laboratory experiment using program code. In *Proceedings of the 6th European Conference Held Jointly with the 5th ACM SIGSOFT international Symposium on Foundations of Software Engineering* (Zurich, Switzerland, September 22 - 25, 1997). M. Jazayeri and H. Schauer, Eds. Foundations of Software Engineering. Springer-Verlag New York, New York, NY, 294-309.

[9] Frank W. Blakely, Mark E. Boles, Hewlett-Packard Journal, Volume 42, Number 4, Oct 1991, pages 58-63. Quoting and copying herein is by permission of the Hewlett-Packard Company.

This pilot study involved a single project with 30 development hours and 20 review hours — 13 hours in pre-meeting inspection and 7 hours in meetings. They restricted their inspection sizes to 200 lines of code per hour as per the guidelines set out by Fagan and Gilb. 21 defects were uncovered giving the project a defect rate of 0.7 per hour and a defect density of 100 per thousand lines of code.

This study went further than most to quantify how many defects found in code review would not have been otherwise found in testing/QA. After all, if you're trying to reduce overall defect numbers, it's not worth spending all this time in review if testing will uncover the problems anyway.

Because they knew this issue was important from the start, they collected enough information on each defect to determine whether each could have been detected had the testing/QA process been better. In particular, for each defect they answered this question: "Is there any test that QA could have reasonably performed that would have uncovered this defect?" Perhaps it would be more efficient to beef up testing rather than reviewing code.

The result was conclusive: Only 4 of the 21 defects could conceivably been caught during a test/QA phase. They further postulate that it would have taken more total engineering hours to find and fix those 4 in QA rather than in inspection.

Dunsmore 2000: Object-Oriented Inspections[10]

What inspection techniques should be used when reviewing object-oriented code? Object-oriented (OO) code has different structural and execution patterns than procedural code; does this imply code review techniques should also be changed, and how so?

---

[10] Dunsmore, A., Roper, M., Wood, M. Object-Oriented Inspection in the Face of Delocalisation, appeared in Proceedings of the 22nd International Conference on Software Engineering (ICSE) 2000, pp. 467-476, June 2000.

Alastair Dunsmore, Marc Roper, and Murray Wood sought to answer this question in a series of experiments.

The first experiment with 47 participants uncovered the first problem with traditional code inspections: Understanding a snippet of OO code often requires the reader to visit other classes in the package or system. Indeed, a large number of defects were rarely found by the reviewers because the defect detection required knowledge outside the immediate code under inspection. With traditional sit-down with code-in-hand inspections the readers didn't have the tools to investigate other classes, and therefore had a hard time finding the defects.

They explored a way to address this problem in the second experiment. The reviewers were given a reading plan that directed their attention to the code in a certain order and supplied additional information according to a systematic set of rules. The rules were a rough attempt at pulling in related code given the code under review. The theory was that, if this technique was better, one could conceivably make a tool to collect the information automatically. This "systematic review" was performed by 64 reviewers and the results compared with those from the first study.

The systematic review was better. Some defects that weren't found by anyone in the first test were found in the second. Furthermore, both reviewers and the creators of the reading plan reported that they enjoyed creating and having the plan because it led to a deeper understanding of the code at hand. Indeed, the plans could be used as documentation for the code even outside the context of a code review. Reviewers also reported feeling more comfortable having a strict reading plan rather than having to wade through a complex change and "wander off" into the rest of the system.

In the third experiment, the researchers compared three different approaches to the review problem in a further attempt to identify what techniques work best in the OO context:

1. The "checklist review" gives the reviewers a specific list of things to check for at the class, method, and class-hierarchy levels. The checklist was built using the experience of the first two experiments as a guide for what types of problems reviewers should be looking for.

2. The "systematic review" technique of the second experiment, with more refinement.

3. The "use-case review" gives the reviewers a set of ways in which one would expect the code to be used by other code in the system. This is a kind of checklist that the code behaves in documented ways, "plays nice" when under stress, and works in a few specific ways that we know will be exercised in the current application.

The result of this experiment is shown in Figure 6. Clearly the checklist method was the most successful, uncovering more defects in less time than the other two techniques, 30% better than the worst in the rate at which defects were uncovered. However it should be mentioned that the defects found in each of the three techniques didn't overlap completely. The authors therefore suggested using more than one approach to over the most ground, although the amount of pre-review time it would take to prepare for all these techniques is probably prohibitive.

In this third experiment they also kept track of the exact time that each of the defects were found during the inspection. Are most defects found quickly? Is there a drop-off point after which defects are no longer found? Is there a difference between the three types of review?

The results are shown in Figure 7.

	Checklist	Systematic	Use-Case
Defects (of 14)	7.3	6.2	5.7
False-Positives	3.4	3.2	2.9
Inspection Time	72.1	77.0	81.9
Defect Rate	6.07	4.83	4.18

Figure 6: Comparing results from three types of reviews. Inspection time is in minutes. Defect rate is in defects per hour.

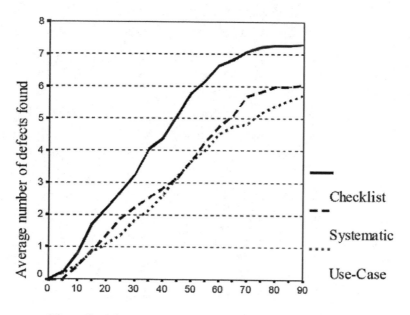

Figure 7: Elapsed time versus cumulative number of defects found for each of the three types of review.

The defect rate is constant until about 60 minutes into the inspection at which point it levels off with no defects found at all after 90 minutes.

In all three review types the pattern is the same. Defects are found at relatively constant rates through the first 60 minutes of inspection. At that point the checklist-style review levels off sharply; the other review styles level off slightly later. In no case is a defect discovered after 90 minutes.

This is direct and conclusive evidence that reviews should be limited to around one hour, not to exceed two hours.

Uwano 2006: Analysis of eye movements during review[11]

Four researchers at the Nara Institute of Science and Technology have completed a unique study of the eye movements of a reviewer during a code review. It's always both fascinating and eerie to get a glimpse into our subconscious physiological behaviors.

It turns out that certain eye scanning patterns during review correlate with being better at finding the defect. Although this is not really something you can teach someone, it does point out ways in which source code could be organized to facilitate comprehension. That is, specific coding standards could make it easier for developers to understand code in general and for reviewers to find defects in particular.

The researchers used a custom-built system that displayed a short C-language program on a screen while an eye scanner recorded all "fixations" – times when the eye stayed within a 30 pixel radius for longer than 1/20th of a second. Furthermore, because they controlled the display of the source code, fixations were matched up with line numbers. The result is a plot of which line of code was looked at over time.

---

[11] Uwano, H., Nakamura, M., Monden, A., and Matsumoto, K. 2006. Analyzing individual performance of source code review using reviewers' eye movement. In *Proceedings of the 2006 Symposium on Eye Tracking Research & Applications* (San Diego, California, March 27 - 29, 2006). ETRA '06. ACM Press, New York, NY, 133-140 © 2006 ACM, Inc. Figures reprinted by permission.

```
01 void main(void){
02 int i, num, isPrime = 0;
03
04 printf("Input Number:");
05 scanf("%d", &num);
06
07 i = 2;
08 while(i < num){
09 if(num%i == 0)
10 isPrime = 1;
11 i = i + 1;
12 }
13
14 if(isPrime == 1)
15 printf("%d is prime number.\n", num);
16 else
17 printf("%d is NOT prime number.\n", num);
18 }
```

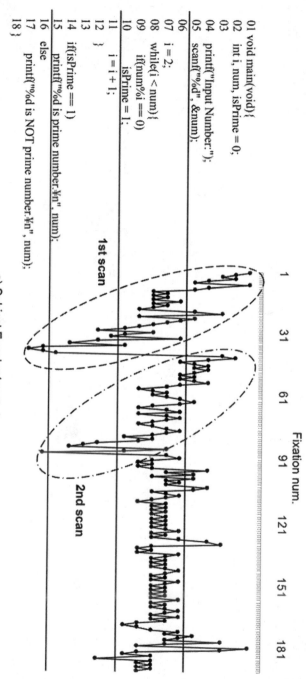

a) Subject E reviewing `Prime`

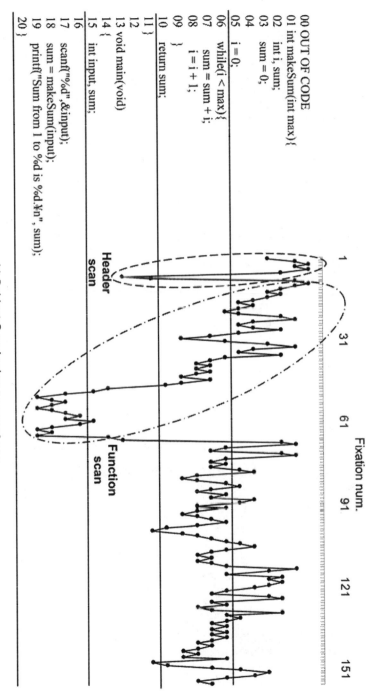

b) Subject C reviewing Accumulate

Six different C snippets were used, each between 12 and 23 lines, each an entire function or small set of functions viewable without scrolling. Five subjects were subjected to each snippet yielding 27 trials (three of the 30 had to be discarded because the subject was distracted during the trial).

The general pattern is the reviewer would read lines from top to bottom in a "bumpy slope." That is, generally straight-through but with short, brief "back-tracks" along the way. They called this the "first scan." Typically 80% of the lines are "touched" during this first scan. Then the reviewer concentrates on a particular portion of the code – 4 or 5 lines – presumably where the reviewer believed the problem was most likely to be.

Other patterns were observed depending on the nature of the code. For example, with code examples containing two functions instead of one, frequently there was a very fast "header scan" where the eyes rested on function declaration lines before the usual "first scan" began. It was also common to see a second scan similar to the first before the concentration begins.

Closer inspection of the eye movements reveals interesting insights into how anyone reads source code for comprehension. For example, the eyes rest on initial variable declarations consistently throughout the session. The mind needs a constant refresher on what these variables mean. Even when there are only two or three local variables, all integers, nothing special or difficult to retain, the pattern is the same. The researchers called this eye movement "retrace declaration." What this means for code structure is that local variable declarations should also be visible on the same screen as code that uses them. Otherwise the reader will have to scroll back and forth. A common way to enforce this is to limit the number of lines of code in a function. We've all heard the arguments for limiting function length for general readability; here's evidence that cements that notion.

As another example, loops have a tremendous fixation rate, far more even than other control structures such as conditionals. Perhaps this is partly a function of the review task – loops are a common location for errors and just the fact that a section of code repeats makes it more difficult to analyze. The lesson for coding standards is that loop conditionals should be as simple as possible. For example, avoid setting variables inside the conditional and try to simplify complex compound Boolean expressions.

But back to reviews. The researchers had initially set out to answer the question: Is there anything about eye movements that can be correlated with review effectiveness or efficiency? The answer turned out to be yes.

There is a negative correlation between the amount of time it takes for the "first scan" and defect detection speed. That is, the more time the reviewer spends during that "first scan" period, the *faster* the reviewer will be at finding the defect. This seems contradictory – the reviewer spends more time scanning the code, yet he finds the defect faster than someone who doesn't bother.

The key is that it's the first, preliminary scan that the reviewer must spend more time on. When a reviewer doesn't take enough time to go through the code carefully, he doesn't have a good idea of where the trouble spots are. His first guess might be off – he might have completely missed a section that would have set off warning bells. The reviewer that takes more time with the initial scan can identify all the trouble spot candidates and then address each one with a high probability of having selected the right area of code to study.

This result has a few ramifications. First, slow down! As we talked about in the conclusion section, the longer you take in review, the more defects you'll find. Haste makes waste.

Second, a preliminary scan is a useful technique in code review. This experiment demonstrates that a reasonably careful "first scan" actually increases defect detection rates.

Laitenberger 1999: Factors affecting number of defects[12]

Under what circumstances would we expect to find more or fewer defects during a review? Does the size of the code under inspection matter? How about the amount of time reviewers spend looking at it? What about the source code language or the type of program?

All of these things are "a factor," but can we state something stronger than that? Perhaps some things matter more than others.

In 1999, three researchers performed an analysis of 300 reviews from Lucent's Product Realization Center for Optical Networking (PRC-ON) in Nuremberg, Germany. This group spends 15% of their total development time in reviews, but were they using their time wisely? Were they detecting as many defects per hour as possible? If not, what specifically should they do to maximize the defect detection rate?

These were the questions Laitenberger set out to answer. A survey of other studies suggested the two most likely factors in the number of defects found during a review: (a) time spent in preparation, and (b) the size of the code under inspection. So they came up with a causal model – that is, a theoretical model of how they expected these two factors might influence the number of defects. This model is shown in Figure 8.

But drawing a diagram doesn't prove anything! How can we test whether this model is accurate and how can we measure just how important each of those causal links are?

---

[12] Evaluating a Causal Model of Review Factors in an Industrial Setting. Oliver Laitenberger, Marek Leszak, Dieter Stoll, and Khaled El-Emam, National Research Council Canada.

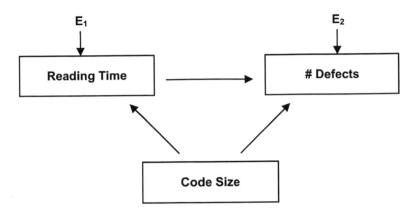

Figure 8: Causal model for the two largest factors that determine the number of defects found during review.

Arrows indicate a causal link. The "E" values represent external factors not accounted for by the model.

As you might expect, there's a statistical system that can do exactly this. It's called Path Analysis. Given the model above and raw data from the individual reviews, we can determine how much each of those arrows really matter[13].

---

13 Each review contains three pieces of data: code size, reading time, and number of defects. Then each of those variables is compared pair-wise; the beta coefficient from a logarithmic least-squares analysis is used as the measure of the pair-wise correlation strength. Correlations must be significant at the 0.01 level to be accepted.

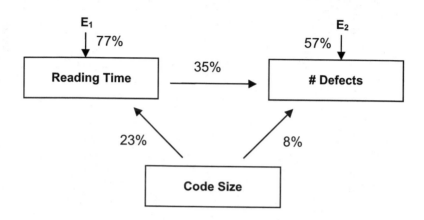

Figure 9: Results of Laitenberger's path analysis for code reviews. Numbers represent percent of total influence.

Results are similar for design and specification reviews.

The results are shown in Figure 9. There are two important things to notice.

First, reading time is twice as influential as code size[14]. This is unexpected – with more code under the magnifying glass you would expect to find more defects. But in fact it's the amount of

---

[14] It may appear that reading time influence is four times larger than code size $(35 \div 8)$, but note that code size also influences reading time, thereby indirectly influencing number of defects through that path. Thus the total code size influence is $0.08 + 0.23*0.35 = 16\%$.

time you spend looking at the code – no matter how big or small the code is – that determines how many defects you find.

Second, the "external factors" are far more important than any of the others. Code size alone predicts only 8% of the variation in number of defects found; reading time predicts 35%, but most of the variation comes from elsewhere. Reviews of new code are different than maintenance code. Complex algorithms differ from complex object relationships which differ from simple procedural code. Languages differ. The experience level of the author and reviewer matters. These external effects collectively constitute the most important factor in how many defects you can expect to find during a review.

This has several implications. First, if you want to find more defects, spend more time reviewing. You could also reduce the amount of code under inspection, but that's less important. Even though various external factors are collectively more influential, the individual reviewer often cannot control those factors; reading time is something that can be controlled directly.

Second, you cannot average all your metrics and say "We should find X defects per 1000 lines of code." Each project, language, module, even class could be different. It might be worth breaking your metrics down at these levels in an attempt to find some real patterns.

Ultimately the most influential variable that you can actually control in your review process is inspection time. That's the knob you turn when you want to find more defects.

Conclusions

Each study in this survey has a different story to tell and uncovers unique insights in the process, but what general information can be gleaned from the literature?

<u>Review for at most one hour at a time.</u>

Although not every study addressed this issue, a common result is that reviewers' effectiveness at finding defects drops off precipitously after one hour. This is true no matter how much material is being reviewed at once. Some studies specifically test for this, seeing how many defects are discovered after 15, 30, 45, 60, 75, 90, and 120 minutes devoted to the task. In all cases there is roughly linear increase in number of defects found up to one hour, then a significant leveling-off after that. This result has been echoed in other studies not covered by this survey.

Study	Review Minutes
Dunsmore, 2000	60
Blakely, 1991	90
Cohen, 2006	90

Figure 10: Cut-off point where further review produced no (significant) benefit.

There are at least two explanations for this effect. First, each reviewer is capable of finding only a certain set of defects. No matter how long you stare at the code, there are some problems that you just don't know how to find. This is especially true if the review is being driven by checklist – the reviewer often focuses on the checklist and anything significantly outside that list is not in scope.

The second explanation is that after an hour the human mind becomes saturated. The reviewer cannot process more possibilities because his brain refuses to concentrate. "I've been looking at this for too long. I'm sick of it" is a common complaint during extended reviews. This second point could be tested by having reviewers return to the code the next day to see if the same person can find more defects after a "reset." No study did this, however, and perhaps it doesn't matter because taking that much time is impractical.

To detect more defects, slow down code readings.

The more time spent in review, the more defects are detected. This might sound obvious; what's not obvious is that this is by far the dominant factor in the number of defects detected.

This is also true whether or not your private code readings are followed up by an inspection meeting.

Inspection meetings need not be in person.

For the sensitive reader accustomed to institutional formal inspections descended from the legacy of Fagan, Gilb, and Wiegers, this statement is heresy. Traditionally the in-person moderator-directed inspection meeting is considered the lynchpin of a successful process. The synergy[15] arising from a properly-conducted meeting produces results that could never be obtained by any reviewer individually, even with training.

In the past fifteen years this effect has been questioned in many studies and from many perspectives. Several conclusions on this point are clear from all the studies in this survey and many others.

First, the vast majority of defects are found in the pre-meeting private "reading" phase. By the time the meeting starts, all questionable aspects of the code are already identified. This makes sense; it would be difficult to determine whether a complex algorithm was implemented correctly by discussion rather than by concentrated effort.

---

[15] Fagan's evocative "phantom inspector."

Second, the primary result of a meeting is in sifting through and possibly removing false-positives – that is, "defects" found during private code readings which turn out to not actually be defects. Even then, false-positives are often the result of poorly documented or organized code; if a reader is confused, perhaps the code should be changed anyway to avoid future confusion, even if this just means introducing better code comments.

The result is that short meetings with just a few participants (or even just the author and a single reviewer) appear to provide the benefits of the inspection meeting (identifying false-positives and knowledge transfer) while keeping inspection rates high (not wasting time). And these "meetings" are just as effective over e-mail or other electronic communication medium.

<u>Defects per line of code are unreliable.</u>

It's the forecaster's dream. How many defects are lurking in these 5000 lines of code? No problem, just take our standard number of defects per kLOC during review and multiply. 12 defects/kLOC? Expect to find 60 defects. If you've only found 30 so far, keep looking.

Unfortunately, this is a pipe dream. Studies agree to disagree: this ratio is all over the map. It is possible that more careful study broken out by file type, project, team, or type of application might reveal better numbers[16]. But for now, give up the quest for the "industry standard" density of defects.

---

[16] Our own in-depth analysis of 2500 reviews revealed two significant factors: time spent in review (more time increased defect density) and author preparation comments (reduced defect density). See that essay in this collection for details.

Study	Defects/kLOC
Kelly 2003	0.27
Laitenberger 1999	7.00
Blakely 1991	105.28
Cohen 2006	10-120

Figure 11: Defects per 1000 lines of code as reported by various studies. The pattern is... there is no pattern.

Omissions are the hardest defects to find.

It's easy to call out problems in code you're staring at; it's much more difficult to realize that something isn't there at all.

Although most studies mentioned this, none measured this problem specifically. The informal consensus is that a checklist is the single best way to combat the problem; the checklist reminds the reviewer to take the time to look for something that might be missing.

For example, in our own experience the utility of a checklist item like "make sure all errors are handled" is of limited usefulness – this is an obvious thing to check for in all code. But we forgot to kick the build number before a QA session started about 30% of the time. After installing a release checklist we haven't forgotten since.

Studies are too small.

An unfortunate common element to these studies is that they are almost all too small to have statistical significance. It's rare to find more than 100 reviews or 100 defects in any of them. Most are along the lines of "In our 21 reviews, we found that..." Twenty-one reviews are not statistically significant, no matter what data you collect!

This doesn't completely invalidate the studies; it just means that we need to consider all of the studies in aggregate, not any one by itself. Also, in each the authors make observations which are interesting and relevant regardless of the metrics they collected.

Study	# Participants	Review Hours	# Defects
Uwano 2006	5	2.5	6
Blakely 1991	*N/A*	7.6	21
Conradi 2003	10	17.3	64
Kelly 2003	7	48.0	147
Dunsmore 2000	64	58.0	7
Laitenberger 1999	*N/A*	*N/A*	3045

Figure 12: Various statistics from each study when available.

The small numbers show that almost none of the studies are large enough by themselves to be statistically significant.

So now lets move from small experiments to the largest case study of lightweight peer review ever published.

Code Review at Cisco Systems

The largest case study ever done on lightweight code review process; data and lessons.

In May of 2006 Smart Bear Software wrapped up a 10-month case study of peer code review in the Cisco MeetingPlace[1] product group at Cisco Systems, Inc[2]. With 2500 reviews of 3.2 million lines of code written by 50 developers, this is the largest case study ever done on what's known as a "lightweight" code review process.

The subject of almost all published literature on code review is of formal, heavyweight meeting-based inspections. But in recent years many development organizations have shrugged off the yoke of meeting schedules, paper-based code readings, and tedious

---

[1] At the time of this writing (June 2006) Cisco is running television ads in America touting the advantages of their teleconferencing solution. This is the story of that development group.

[2] Cisco® and MeetingPlace® are registered trademarks of Cisco Systems Inc.. These names and the information herein are reproduced with permission.

metrics-gathering in favor of new lightweight review processes. Certain lightweight processes appear to have the same proven benefits and measurability found in heavyweight processes while drastically reducing total time spent engaged in procedures.

The studies in the previous chapter have already suggested that formal meetings add hours to the process without uncovering additional defects. Furthermore we have found that most developers prefer a faster, more lightweight approach, and managers like the idea of a process nimble enough to be applied to all code changes across the board, not just those dangerous enough to warrant the time investment of a formal inspection.

But you cannot sacrifice code quality. You cannot just throw away 30 years of evidence that heavyweight process works. Where are the numbers to support the effectiveness of a lightweight process, and what guidelines should be followed to ensure an effective review?

The Smart Bear / Cisco study sought to answer exactly those questions. We used real developers working on commercially-available software at an established software company; no students, no contrived code snippets, no sterile laboratory conditions.

Cisco has a long history of using various types of code review as part of their legendary quality control. The MeetingPlace group was no exception. In July 2005, 50 developers in the MeetingPlace group started using a software tool for lightweight review in the hopes that it would increase defect detection while speeding up overall review time and removing some of the drudgery normally associated with inspections.

We'll analyze the results of those reviews and determine the general characteristics of effective, efficient reviews under this system. In the process we will demonstrate that this particular brand of lightweight review is able to uncover as many defects with as many process metrics in much less time than heavyweight formal inspections.

How reviews were conducted

The reviews were conducted using Smart Bear Software's Code Collaborator system for tool-assisted peer review. Code Collaborator is described in detail and with screenshots in another essay in this collection; here we'll only summarize the process.

Cisco wanted a review before every code change was checked into the version control server, which in their case was Perforce®. They used a Perforce server trigger (included with Code Collaborator) that prevented any code check-in unless a review existed in the Code Collaborator server, and that review was "complete" with all found defects fixed and verified.

Software developers were provided with several Code Collaborator tools allowing them to upload local changes from the command-line, a Windows GUI, or from a plug-in to the Perforce GUI clients P4Win and P4V.

Reviews were performed using Code Collaborator's web-based user interface. Authors determined who was "invited" to be a reviewer or observer; about half the reviews had a single reviewer, the rest two or more. Invitations were sent by Code Collaborator via e-mail.

During the inspection, Code Collaborator presented before/after difference views to all participants. Everyone could comment on any line of code by clicking on the line and typing. Comments are kept threaded and are always visible next to the code in question (see Figure 13).

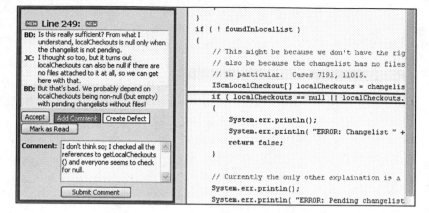

Figure 13: Code Collaborator screenshot showing threaded comments next to Java code under inspection. The author is defending a design decision.

Defects are logged like comments, also threaded by file and line number. When an author believed a defect had been fixed, the new files were uploaded to the same review. The web interface then presents these new changes against the original so reviews can verify that defects were fixed and no new defects opened. This back-and-forth process happens as many times as is necessary for all defects to be fixed.

Once all reviewers agree the review is complete and no defects are still open, the review is complete and the author is then allowed to check the changes into Perforce.

Code Collaborator automatically gathers key review metrics such as man-hours spent in review and lines of code under inspection. It is these metrics, combined with defect logs, that we analyze below.

Thinning the herd

Some reviews in the sample set reflect special cases that we don't wish to analyze in general. There are two specific cases we want to throw out of the analysis:

1. Reviews of enormous amounts of code. If many thousands of lines of code were under review, we can be sure this is not a true code review.

2. Trivial reviews. These are reviews in which clearly the reviewer never looked at the code, or at least not long enough for any real effect. For example, if the entire review took two seconds, clearly no review actually took place.

We can visualize these cases by considering a plot of "lines of code under inspection" against "inspection rate in lines per hour." From the log-log chart in Figure 14 it is apparent that there are aberrant data points for both enormous LOC and enormous inspection rates.

There are some clear cut-off points for rejecting samples given the data in Figure 14. For example, a 10,000 line-per-hour inspection rate implies the reviewer can read and understand source code at a rate of three lines per second. As another example, a single review of 10,000 lines of code isn't possible. It is also apparent that the majority of reviews appear in much more reasonable ranges.

There are several explanations for these outliers. Because review was required before version control check-in, large unreviewed changes will still pass through the system. This explains for example the reviews of many tens of thousands of lines which are reviewed too quickly to be careful inspections.

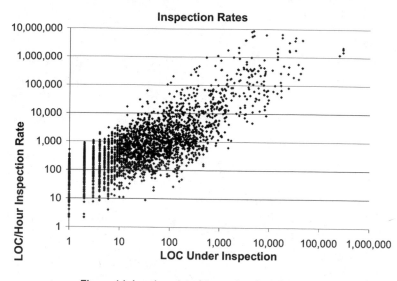

Figure 14: Log-log plot of lines of code (LOC) under inspection versus the speed of inspection (in
LOC per hour).

The columnar grouping pattern for small LOC is a
result of the LOC variable being an integer and
the logarithmic scale expanding that region.

There are also cases of reasonable inspection sizes reviewed
faster than is humanly possible. One explanation is the pass-
through review – the reviewer simply OK's the changes without
looking at them. Another explanation is that the reviewer and
developer communicated about this review outside the system, so
by the time the official review came around the reviewer didn't
need to look at the code. In either case we are not interested in
data from these lightning-fast reviews.

We therefore make the following rules about throwing out
reviews from the study:

1. Throw out reviews whose total duration is shorter than 30 seconds.
2. Throw out reviews where the inspection rate is greater than 1500 LOC/hour.
3. Throw out reviews where the number of lines under review is greater than 2000.

This attempt at isolating "interesting" review cases cuts out 21% of the reviews. The distribution in Figure 15 shows that the most reviews are smaller than 200 lines of code and are inspected slower than 500 LOC/hour.

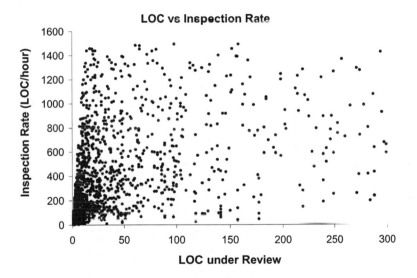

Figure 15: Distribution of reviews after discarding those that cannot represent proper reviews. Most reviews are under 150 lines of code and reviewed slower than 500 LOC/hour.

Inspection Rate Analysis

How fast should code be reviewed? If you go too fast you're liable to miss defects. Industry experts say inspection rates should not exceed 200 lines per hour if you want an effective review. Does review rate differ by reviewer or author or the type of code under inspection?

We might expect a relatively constant inspection rate. That is, it should take twice as long to review 200 lines of code than it does to review 100 lines of code. In general, if we plot code size versus time-to-review, we expect the values to cluster around a line that represents the average review rate. However, Figure 16 shows this is not the case. No clustering around a common rate, not even when we zoom in on the "cluster" of data with reviews under one hour and under 200 lines.

Although this result is unexpected, it's great news for our analysis. It means that in this experiment review inspection rates and sizes vary over a wide range of values, which means we have a good sampling of data to use when answering questions like "Does inspection rate or inspection size affect the number of defects found?" or "What inspection rate makes the reviewer most efficient at finding defects?"

Indeed, the next logical question is: "What are the factors that determine the inspection rate?" Do detail-oriented reviewers agonize over every line? Does the guy with empty Red Bull cans all over his cubicle race through code? Do certain files or modules take longer to review?

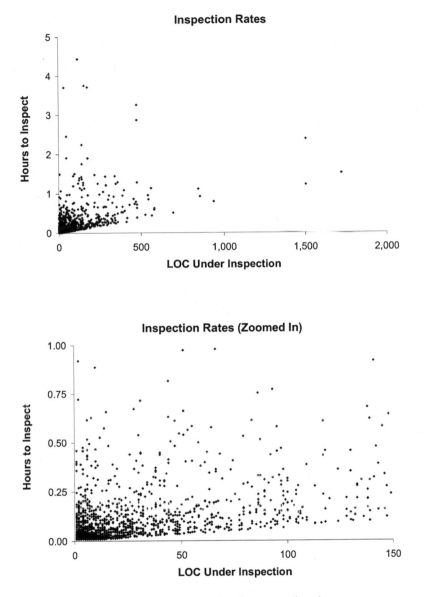

Figure 16: Plotting inspection size versus time, in
total and zoomed into the cluster near the origin.
There is no apparent systematic "inspection rate."
The absence of data points below the invisible line
with slope 1/1500 is due to our throwing out
reviews with high inspection rates.

Does the inspection rate vary by reviewer?

Do some reviewers zoom through code while others linger? Do your star developers take longer because they are given the hardest code to review? Does the identity of the reviewer make the inspection rate predictable?

Unfortunately the assumptions of ANOVA[3] are not met for these data, so we investigated individual reviewer rates by hand. A typical example is shown in Figure 17 for Reviewer #3. Clearly this reviewer has no one rate[4].

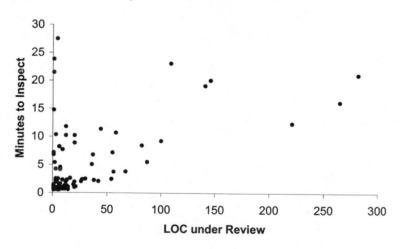

Figure 17: An analysis of inspection rate for Reviewer #3 shows there is no single rate and identifies some interesting special cases along the y-axis.

---

[3] ANalysis Of VAriance – the standard statistical technique for determining the relative influence of many independent variables on a dependent variable.
[4] The best-fit rate is only $R^2 = 0.29$.

We did notice something odd. There are four reviews of 1 or 2 lines of code that each took over 15 minutes to complete. The other reviews that took that long had over 100 lines of code! These might these be aberrant, and removing aberrant data points might give us a statistically significant inspection rate. So we took a closer look.

Each of these outlier cases was explainable. In one case, a separate review contained the real changes; the reviewer had simply referred back to the first frequently while looking at the second. In all other cases there was a lot of dialog between the reviewer and the author or other reviewers. These code modifications, though small in physical size, all seemed to have significant ramifications for the rest of the system according to the comments.

So after close inspection it was clear that these data points did belong in our data set. And this in turn means that there still is not a clear inspection rate.

Another feature of the single-reviewer graphs (e.g. Figure 17) is the cluster of small-change, fast reviews near the origin, just as we saw with the global inspection rate graphs. And once again, when we zoomed into that area alone it was clear that no particular rule governs inspection rate, even for a single reviewer (see Figure 18).

But occasionally we found a reviewer who seemed to have a more regular inspection rate. Figure 19 shows one example with a decent inspection rate correlation. However these were rare and usually associated with reviewers who hadn't participated in many reviews yet; presumably as they encountered more types of source code they too would start to show a larger spread.

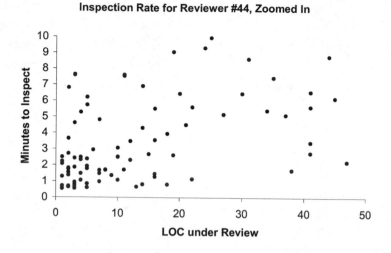

Figure 18: Another example showing no pattern in inspection rate even when zoomed into the mass of data points near the origin.

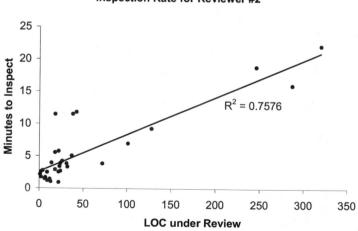

Figure 19: Example of a reviewer who appears to have a consistent inspection rate.

Does the inspection rate vary by author?

So the reviewer doesn't determine the rate, but perhaps the author does. Different authors work on different modules and types of code. Some authors might write code that takes longer to read.

Again, we find the same results (Figure 20): No linear relationship, clustering around the origin.

The column of data points at LOC=141 needs to be explained. This is review #1174 which happened to have six different (and simultaneous) reviewers. Each participant took a different amount of time to examine the code and talk about it with the others.

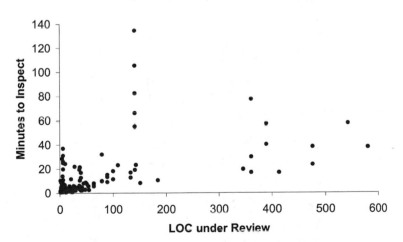

Figure 20: No pattern in per-author inspection rates. The column of points at LOC=141 is explained in the text.

In fact, review #1174 constitutes additional evidence that inspection rate doesn't depend on the reviewer. All six reviewers were examining and chatting about a single review, yet the amount of time spent during the review varied widely.

Conclusion for inspection rate

We found no metric that correlated significantly with inspection rate. It is clear that many factors combine to determine the speed at which a reviewer will scan a set of code changes.

But none of this means all these reviews were equally effective or efficient at finding defects. The literature suggests that slow inspections uncover more defects. But before we can explore review effectiveness we first need to decide what constitutes a "defect."

Counting Defects

What is a "defect?" Before we get into defect rate and density analysis we need to define exactly what a "defect" means and how we will identify defects in our sample data here.

Although the word "defect" has an inherent negative connotation, in code review it is defined in this way:

When a reviewer or consensus of reviewers determines that code must be changed before it is acceptable, it is a "defect." If the algorithm is wrong, it's a defect. If the code is right but unintelligible due to poor documentation, it's a defect. If the code is right but there's a better way to do it, it's a defect. A simple conversation is not a defect nor is a conversation where a reviewer believed he found a defect but later agreed that it wasn't one. In any event a defect is an improvement to the code that would not have occurred without review.

Counting defects in Code Collaborator should be easy in theory because the software includes a built-in defect logging system that not only logs defects against files and line numbers but also allows for a selection of severity and type. Unfortunately this theory does not apply with this data.

In particular, reviewers and authors are free to communicate the existence of a defect without creating a proper defect record in the database. Furthermore, with earlier versions of the software the workflow surrounding defects was confusing, so the path of least resistance was to talk about defects but not necessarily to open them.

Therefore we cannot just use the defect data from the database as a true measure of defects. Instead we took a random sample of 300 reviews and studied the conversations in each one to measure the number of true defects as defined above.

Defect Density Analysis

Almost all code review process analysts want to measure "defect density," meaning the number of defects found per 1000 lines of code. This number is often associated with review "effectiveness" in that a more effective review will uncover more defects per line of code compared with a cursory review. In a predictive capacity, the density number allows us to answer questions like "How many defects will we expect code review to uncover in 10,000 lines of code?"

Our reviews had an average 32 defects per 1000 lines of code. 61% of the reviews uncovered no defects; of the others the defect density ranged evenly between 10 and 130 defects per kLOC.

Defect density and review size

The relationship between defect density and the amount of code under review is made clear by Figure 21.

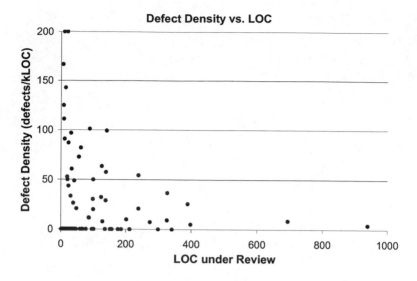

Figure 21: As the amount of code under review
increases reviewers become less effective at finding defects assuming a constant true number of
defects per kLOC.

Reviewers are most effective at reviewing small amounts of
code. Anything below 200 lines produces a relatively high rate of
defects, often several times the average. After that the results trail
off considerably; no review larger than 250 lines produced more
than 37 defects per 1000 lines of code[5].

<hr />

[5] The critical reader will notice we're tacitly assuming that true defect density is
constant over both large and small code changes. That is, we assume a 400-line
change necessarily contains four times the number of defects in a 100-line
change, and thus if defect densities in code review fall short of this the review
must be "less effective." Current literature generally supports this assumption
although there are clearly cases where we would naturally expect large code
changes to have fewer defects per line, e.g. a new class interface with detailed
documentation and no executable code.

These results are not surprising. If the reviewer is overwhelmed with a large quantity of code he won't give the same attention to every line as he might with a small change. He won't be able to explore all the ramifications of the change in a single sitting.

Another explanation comes from the well-established fact that after 60 minutes reviewers "wear out" and stop finding additional defects[6]. Given this, a reviewer will probably not be able to review more than 300-400 lines of code before his performance drops.

But this hypothesis is more directly measurable by considering the inspection rate.

Defect density and inspection rate

It makes sense that reviewers hurried through a review won't find as many defects. A fast inspection rate might mean the reviewer didn't take enough time, or it could mean the reviewer couldn't give enough time for the large quantity of code under review.

The "slower is better" hypothesis is confirmed in Figure 22. Reviewers slower than 400 lines per hour were above average in their ability to uncover defects. But when faster than 450 lines/hour the defect density is below average in 87% of the cases.

---

[6] A compelling example of this is given in the survey of case studies essay elsewhere in this collection.

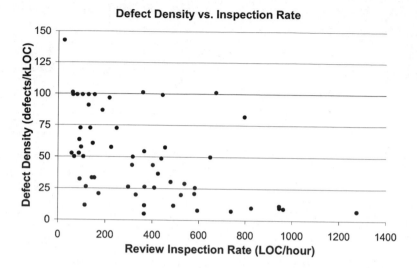

Figure 22: Reviewers become less effective at finding defects as their pace through the review accelerates.

Defect density and author preparation

Could authors eliminate most defects before the review even begins? If we required developers to double-check their work, maybe reviews could be completed faster without compromising code quality. We were able to test this technique at Cisco.

The idea of "author preparation" is that authors should annotate their source code before the review begins. Annotations guide the reviewer through the changes, showing which files to look at first and defending the reason and methods behind each code modification. The theory is that because the author has to re-think all the changes during the annotation process, the author will himself uncover most of the defects before the review even begins, thus making the review itself more efficient. Reviewers will uncover problems the author truly would not have thought of otherwise.

If author preparation has a real effect it will be to reduce the number of defects found during the inspection. This means a *lower defect density* because in theory the author has already removed most of the defects.

So we tested the hypothesis: "Reviews with author preparation have smaller defect densities compared to reviews without." It is easy to detect "author preparation" in our data because we record every comment, threaded by file and line of code. Without author preparation, conversations are typically started by a reviewer or observer and often answered by the author. Author preparation is signified by the author kicking off the conversation. In our manual scan of reviews we found almost no cases where the author started the conversation and yet wasn't prepping the reviewer.

The relationship between author preparation and defect density is shown in Figure 23. The data supports our hypothesis in two specific ways. First, for all reviews with at least one author preparation comment, defects density is never over 30; in fact the most common case is for there to be no defects at all! Second, reviews without author preparation comments are all over the map whereas author-prepared reviews do not share that variability.

Clearly author preparation is correlated with low defect densities. But there are at least two ways to explain this correlation, each leading to opposite conclusions about whether author preparation should be mandatory.

Effect of Author Preparation on Defect Density

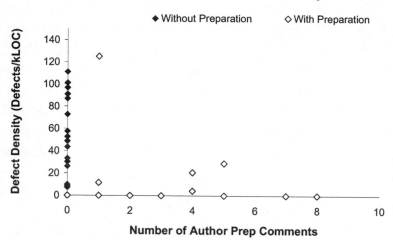

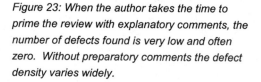

Figure 23: When the author takes the time to prime the review with explanatory comments, the number of defects found is very low and often zero. Without preparatory comments the defect density varies widely.

One conclusion is that the very act of deeply preparing for a review causes the author to identify and correct most defects on his own. The analogous adage is "I read I forget; I see I remember; I teach I understand." We all have personal experience to back this up; when you're forced to explain your work to someone else, anticipating their questions and teaching them your techniques, you uncover things you hadn't thought about before.

The other conclusion is that prepping disables the reviewer's capacity for criticism. Author comments prime the reviewer for what to expect. As long as the code matches the prose, the reviewer is satisfied. Because the reviewer is guided he doesn't think outside the box, doesn't approach the problem fresh, and doesn't bring new insight to the problem. The reason defect density is low for an author-prepared review is not because the author pre-fixed defects, but rather because the reviewers aren't looking hard enough.

We believe the first conclusion is more tenable. A survey of the reviews in question show the author is being conscientious, careful, and helpful, and not misleading the reviewer. Often the reviewer will respond or ask a question or open a conversation on another line of code, demonstrating that he was not dulled by the author's annotations.

Indeed, we believe these preparation comments belie a fundamental personal development philosophy of attention to detail, consideration of consequences, and general experience. That is, we believe the developers who are naturally meticulous will exhibit this in the form of preparation – it's just another way of expressing their cautious approach. Even with developers who are not naturally this way, we believe that requiring preparation will cause anyone to be more careful, rethink their logic, and write better code overall.

Defect Rate Analysis

Where defect density measures a review's effectiveness, defect rate – defects per hour – measures a review's efficiency. It answers the question "How fast do we uncover defects?"

The overall defect rate was 13 defects per hour with 85% of the reviews slower than 25 defects per hour.

With defect density we determined that large reviews resulted in ineffective reviews. Will a large review also have a detrimental effect on defect rate?

From Figure 24 it is clear that review size does not affect the defect rate. Although the smaller reviews afforded a few especially high rates, 94% of all reviews had a defect rate under 20 defects per hour regardless of review size.

So reviewers are able to uncover problems at a relatively fixed rate regardless of the size of the task put in front of them. In fact, the take-home point from Figure 24 is that defect rate is constant across all the reviews regardless of external factors.

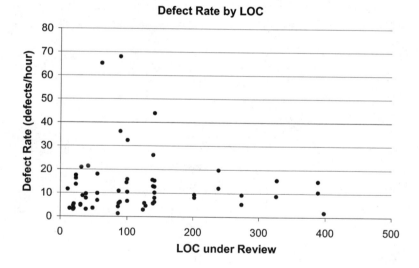

Figure 24: Defect rate is not influenced by the size of the review.

Conclusions

We believe our results allow us to conclude the following:

- LOC under review should be under 200, not to exceed 400. Anything larger overwhelms reviewers and defects are not uncovered.
- Inspection rates less than 300 LOC/hour result in best defect detection. Rates under 500 are still good; expect to miss significant percentage of defects if faster than that.
- Authors who prepare the review with annotations and explanations have far fewer defects than those that do not. We presume the cause to be that authors are forced to self-review the code.
- Total review time should be less than 60 minutes, not to exceed 90. Defect detection rates plummet after that time.
- Expect defect rates around 15 per hour. Can be higher only with less than 175 LOC under review.
- Left to their own devices, reviewers' inspection rate will vary widely, even with similar authors, reviewers, files, and size of the review.

Given these factors, the single best piece of advice we can give is to review between 100 and 300 lines of code at a time and spend 30-60 minutes to review it.

Smaller changes can take less time, but always spend at least 5 minutes, even on a single line of code[7].

Lightweight vs. Heavyweight

How do our results compare with those from heavyweight formal inspections? Were our lightweight inspections less effective at uncovering defects? Did they really take less time?

---

[7] We saw many reviews where a change to a single line of code had ramifications throughout the system.

Some of our results exactly match those from established literature. It is well-established that total review time should be under 90 minutes and that slower inspections yield more defects.

Other results are quite different. Across four of the studies of heavyweight inspections given in the previous chapter the average defect detection rate was 2.6 defects per hour[8]; our reviews were *seven times* faster. This is to be expected since our reviews didn't include two-hour inspection meetings with 3-5 participants.

However the critical reader will point out that faster is only better if the same number of defects were uncovered than would have been under a formal inspection process. Unfortunately because this was a study *in situ* and not in a laboratory, we don't know how each of these reviews would have fared with a different process. We can point to the work of Votta and others from the previous chapter for evidence that the lack of inspection meetings did not significantly decrease the number of reported defects, but we would have preferred to compare trials of the same code reviewed in both ways[9].

In light of these other studies, we conclude that lightweight review using Code Collaborator is probably just as effective and definitely more time-efficient than heavyweight formal inspections.

This is not to say that formal inspections don't have a place in the software development process. Many of our other Code Collaborator customers perform formal inspections instead of or on top of lightweight reviews. But heavyweight process takes too much time to be practical with many code changes; here the lightweight process provides measurable, respectable results fast

---

[8] 0.69 from Blakely 1991, 5.45 from Dunsmore 2000, 1.31 from Conradi 2003, and 3.06 from Kelly 2003.

[9] We cannot give a single number for "expected defect density" for formal inspection because studies differ widely on this point. For example, Blakely 1991 found 105 defects per kLOC where Laitenberger 1999 found 7 and Kelly 2003 only 0.27!

enough to be realistically applied during almost every part of the application development lifecycle.

Future Study

We would like to compare heavyweight and lightweight reviews on the same set of code. We would like to experiment with specific rules of review to see how we might improve defect density or defect rate numbers. Would an enforced minimum inspection-time rule increase defect densities? Would enforcing author preparation comments result in more defects detected in less time? Would reviewer-training result in better defect detection? Would a per-file-type or per-author checklist improve defect detection?

We are currently looking for development groups who would like to participate in future studies where some of these conclusions can be tested directly.

Check with the Smart Bear website for new studies, and please let us know if you would like to participate in one yourself.

Social Effects of Peer Review

Unexpected positive social aspects; handling hurt feelings, and the "Big Brother Effect."

Perhaps a manager's most difficult task is to deal with emotions and human interactions. It's easy to think of Vulcan-like developers having no feelings, but nothing could be farther from the truth, outward appearances notwithstanding.

Any criticism is an opportunity both for growth and for embarrassment. In our experience with customers and with in-house code review we've uncovered several social issues that managers and team-leads should be aware of. Some are positive and should be encouraged in the group; others are negative and need to be addressed in a way that is both sensitive and effective.

The "Ego Effect"

The first effect takes place even before the first code review happens. The ego will inflict both good and bad feelings in code review; in this case good.

"Jerry always forgets to check for NULL-pointer exceptions." No one wants to be known as the guy who always makes silly, junior-level mistakes. So imagine yourself in front of a compiler, tasked with fixing a small bug, but knowing that as soon as you say "I'm finished" your peers – or worse your boss – will be critically examining your work.

How will this change your development style? As you work – certainly before you declare code-complete – you'll be a little more conscientious. Do your comments explain what you did and why? Did you remember to check for invalid input data? Are there a few more unit tests you could write?

In other words, you become a better developer *immediately*.

You're going to do a great job because you want a perfect review report. "Wow," your boss will declare in the meeting notes, "I've never reviewed code that was this thoughtful! I can't think of a single thing to say! Perfect!"

OK, maybe not. But you want the general timbre of behind-your-back conversations to be "Oh yeah, his stuff is pretty tight. He's a good developer" and not "He's pretty good but makes a lot of silly errors. When he says he's done, he's not."

A nice characteristic of the Ego Effect is that it works equally well whether reviews are mandatory for all code changes or just used as "spot-checks." If you have a 1-in-3 chance of being called out for review, that's still enough of an incentive to make sure you do a great job. There is a breaking point, however. For example, if you just had a 1-in-10 chance of getting reviewed, you might be sloppier because now you have an excuse. "Yeah, I usually remember to do that. You just caught me on a bad day."

This is an example of the ego working for us. Later we'll see how the ego can result in social problems, but for now let's stay positive and investigate a fun, productive aspect of peer code review that is rarely pointed out.

Old Habits Die Easy

It was our second code review at Smart Bear Software using an alpha version of our new code review tool. I was reviewing a small change Brandon made to some Java code. He had added the following line of code:

```
if ( "integrate".equals( str ) ) { ... }
```

I stared at it for a moment. He was testing whether a string str was equal to the constant string integrate. But I would have written it the other way — with integrate and str switched. I realized both methods work, but perhaps there was a reason he picked this one?

I shot him a quick message. He explained that if str is null, his way the expression will return false whereas with my way we'd have a null-pointer exception. So he's in the habit of putting constant strings on the left side of an equals() expression like that.

Good trick! A new habit I can get into that will eliminate an entire class of bugs from my code[1]. I just became a slightly better developer. And I had fun doing it!

Later we were talking about the review and we realized two totally unexpected things happened here.

---

[1] As a C developer I was used to the similar trick of putting numeric constants on the left side of double-equal signs in conditions, e.g. if(0==x) rather than if(x==0). This way if I accidentally used a single-equal operator the compiler would complain. The Java example is analogous, and yet somehow my brain didn't make the connection. It just goes to show you're never too old to learn something in computer science!

First, my learning experience had nothing to do with the bug Brandon was fixing. Just the fact that we were communicating about source code meant we were also sharing knowledge.

Second, I was the reviewer, yet I was the one learning something. Normally you think of the review process as unidirectional – the reviewer points out problems for the author, and the author might learn something in the process. But here I was the reviewer, and yet I was the one who was learning!

This was not an isolated incident. In the next four weeks we had all learned a lot from each other – everything from programming tricks to obscure facts about the system API and virtual machine. Our collective insights were spread around quickly – far faster that any other technique we could have invented.

And the best part was: It was fun! It's just plain fun to learn something new and to grow as a developer. And it's fun when everyone else in the office is learning too – it's just as fun to teach as to learn and you get the feeling that the whole development organization is accelerating.

Systematic Personal Growth

It gets even better.

Try this experiment sometime[2]: For one week, make a log of every error you make. Every misspelling in e-mail, every time you accidentally close the application you're working in, every time you have a bug in your code, even every syntax error you make. Don't get too specific; keep each item in the list high-level and use hash marks to count how many times you make that type of mistake.

For now, just imagine you've done this. As you might guess, certain patterns emerge. A few of the items have an awful lot of

---

[2] These ideas were inspired by the Software Engineering Institute's (SEI) Personal Software Process (PSP). This is a collection of methods for increasing personal productivity in concrete, measurable ways.

hash marks next to them. In fact, by the end of the second day you might have been getting tired of counting some of them!

And that annoyance might live in the back of your mind. You might even start thinking about it consciously. Pretty soon you'll anticipate the mistake and prevent yourself from making it. Some of those will come easy, others will take work to eliminate.

But eventually you develop habits that prevent that type of error completely. If you frequently forget to close parenthesis in your code, perhaps you'll enable the feature in your code editor that closes parenthesis for you. If you close applications by accident, maybe you'll pause just a few seconds every time you're about to hit the close button. Maybe you'll look up how to spell common words or learn how to input your common mistakes into the auto-correct facility in your e-mail editor.

Over time you become more productive, more efficient. You're working faster and smarter. Not through some self-help seven-step program, just by observing yourself a little more carefully and systematically than you're used to.

Code review is an opportunity to do exactly this with regard to your software development skills. Reviewers will do the work of determining your typical flaws; all you have to do is keep a short list of the common flaws in your work. Over time, correct them. Pick a few at a time to work on. No pressure, no deadlines, just think about it sometimes.

In fact, this technique works almost as well when you review your own code than when someone else reviews it. Usually you need to at least view the code in a format that isn't your standard editor to get the problems to jump out at you, just as errors in Word documents become clear only when printed instead of viewing on-screen. Indeed, many code inspection advocates insist that inspections must be done only with print-outs for this very reason.

Even if employed informally and irregularly, this technique helps you become a better, more efficient developer by leveraging the feedback you're already getting from peer review. And once again, becoming better is fun!

But of course not all social aspects of code review are fun and personally rewarding. Managers should be aware of these problems and know how to mitigate them.

Hurt Feelings & The "Big Brother" Effect

There are two major ways in which code review adversely affects the social environment of the development team. Fortunately it turns out that one managerial technique can address both problems at once. Here we explain the two problems and give specific ways for managers to address them.

First: Hurt feelings.

No one takes criticism well. Some people blow up more easily than others, but everyone feels a twinge when defects are pointed out. Especially when the subject is trying his hardest, deficiencies pointed out can feel like personal attacks.

Some people can handle it, correct the problem, laugh at their own foibles, and move on, where others takes things personally and retreat to their cubicle to ruminate and tend to their bruised egos.

Second: The "Big Brother" effect.

As a developer you automatically assume it's true. Your review metrics are measured automatically by supporting tools. Did you take too long to review some changes? Are your peers finding too many bugs in your code? How will this affect your next performance evaluation?

Metrics are vital for process measurement, which in turn is the basis of process improvement, but metrics can be used for good or evil. If developers believe their metrics will be used against them, not only will they be hostile to the process, but you should also expect them to behave in a way that (they believe) improves their metrics, rather than in a way that is actually productive.

Of course these feelings and attitudes cannot be prevented completely, but managers can do a lot to mitigate the problem. It can be difficult to notice these problems, so managers have to be proactive.

Singling someone out is more likely to cause more problems than it solves. Even in a private one-on-one conversation it's difficult to give any kind of advice that might temper emotions.

We recommend that managers deal with this by addressing all developers as a group. During any existing meeting, take a few moments to assuage everyone at once using some of the points below. Don't call a special meeting for this – then everyone is uneasy because it seems like there's a problem. Just fold it into a standard weekly status meeting or some other normal procedure.

These points are all ways of explaining that (a) defects are good, not evil and (b) defect density is not correlated with developer ability and that therefore (c) defects shouldn't be shunned and will never be used for performance evaluations.

1. Hard code has more defects

Having many defects doesn't necessarily mean the developer was sloppy. It might be that the code itself was more difficult – intrinsically complex or located in a high-risk module that demands the highest quality code. In fact, the more complex the code gets the more we'd *expect* to find defects, no matter who was writing the code.

Indeed, the best way to look at this is to turn it around: If you knew a piece of code was complicated, and a reviewer said he found no flaws at all, wouldn't you suspect the reviewer of not being diligent? If I presented this essay to an editor, even after multiple passes at self-review, and the editor had no comments at all, shouldn't I suspect the editor of not having read the text?

It's easy to see a sea of red marks and get disheartened; your good hard work is full of flaws. But remember that difficult code is supposed to have flaws; it just means the reviewers are doing their jobs.

2. More time yields more defects

An interesting result of studies in code inspection is that the more time the reviewer spends on the code the more defects are found. In retrospect that might sound obvious – the longer you stare at something the more you can say about it. But the amount of time needed to find all defects is greater than you might guess.

In some cases, the group tried to target a certain amount of time per page of code, testing whether spending 5, 15, 30, or even 60 minutes per page made a difference. Most found increases in defect densities up until at least 30 minutes per page, some even saw increases at 60 minutes per page. After a certain point the number of defects would level off – at some point you really have considered everything you can think of – and further time spent on the code would yield no extra defects. But 60 or even 30 minutes per page is a lot more time than most people would guess.

But what this also means is that the quantity of defects found in a piece of code has more to do with how much time the reviewer spent looking at the code as opposed to how "good" the code was to begin with. Just as more complex code ought to yield more defects, reviewers that spend more time on code ought to uncover more defects. And this still has nothing to do with the author's productivity or ability.

3. It's all about the code

Remind everyone that the goal of this process is to make the code as good as possible. All humans are fallible, and mistakes will be made no matter how careful or experienced you are.

In 1986 the space shuttle Challenger exploded 110.3 seconds after lift-off, killing all seven crew members. The subsequent presidential investigation sought to answer two questions: What caused the explosion, and why wasn't this prevented?

The first question was answered in a famous demonstration by the Nobel Prize-winning physicist Richard Feynman[3]. The answer wasn't incredible; the rubber O-rings used to connect sections of the fuel task were inelastic at low temperatures and therefore allowed fuel to leak out the side of the tank where it subsequently ignited. The troubling part is that this wasn't news. This was a documented, well-understood physical property. So why didn't they cancel the launch?

Suddenly the second question became much more interesting. Not just to figure out whom to blame for the debacle, but to correct systemic problems that impact the safety of all missions.

It got worse. It turns out the rocket engineers *did* report the data that implied that launching at 29 degrees Fahrenheit was unsafe. The data were contained in a report given from rocket engineers to launch officials the night before the launch.

So the launch officials were at fault for authorizing a launch when engineers had data showing it was unsafe? No, because the manner in which the data were presented completely hid the trend that predicts this effect[4]. The raw information was present, but the charts were drawn and data arranged in a manner that completely obscured the key relationship between O-ring failure and launch temperature. Given that presentation, no one would have concluded the launch was unsafe.

---

[3] Feynman dunked a rubber O-ring in a glass of ice water and demonstrated that they became brittle at that temperature – the same temperature as it was at the launch.

[4] A fascinating description of the problem (and a solution that would have prevented this disaster) is given in Edward Tufte's *Visual Explanations: Images and Quantities, Evidence and Narrative.*

So the engineers were at fault for misrepresenting the data? No, because the data were correct. No one thought to re-arrange the data in a manner that would have shown the trend. No one was trained in data visualization and presentation techniques.

The take-home point is this: Even with many, very intelligent and experienced people, mistakes will be made. NASA addressed this problem in nine parts, most of which are forms of review[5]. The point of software code review is the same – to eliminate as many defects as possible, regardless of who "caused" the error, regardless of who found it. This isn't personal.

Indeed, as a manager you know that if "quantity of defects" *were* used in performance evaluations, developers would have incentive to not open defects even when they know they're there. That's the opposite of the goal of the review process, so you know that defects must necessarily not factor into any personal – or personnel – report.

Tell your developers you understand what they're afraid of; then they're more likely to believe that their fears are unfounded.

4. The more defects the better

The preceding points lead to a seemingly illogical conclusion: The more defects we find, the better. After all, if finding a defect means a Challenger disaster is averted, than finding defects is good. If we'd expect defects in important or complex code, finding defects in that code is good. If reviewers naturally find more defects when they're diligent, higher numbers of defects are good.

This conclusion is in fact correct! Think of it this way: Every defect found and fixed in peer review is another bug a customer never saw. Another problem QA didn't spend time tracking down. Another piece of code that doesn't incrementally add to the

---

[5] See the official correspondence between NASA and the Presidential Commission on the Space Shuttle Challenger Accident. http://history.nasa.gov/rogersrep/genindex.htm

unmantainablility of the software. Both developers and managers can sleep a little easier at night every time a defect is uncovered.

The reviewer and the author are a team. Together they intend to produce code excellent in all respects, behaving as documented and easy for the next developer to understand. The back-and-forth of code-and-find-defects is not one developer chastising another – it's a process by which two developers can develop software of far greater quality than either could do alone.

The more defects that are found, the better the team is working together. It doesn't mean the author has a problem; it means they're both successfully exploring all possibilities and getting rid of many mistakes. Authors and reviewers should be *proud* of any stretch of code where many defects were found and corrected.

Also, as described earlier, defects are the path to personal growth. As long as over time you're eliminating your most common types of mistakes, defects are a necessary part of the feedback loop that makes you a better developer. So again, the more defects that are found the better; without that feedback you cannot continue to grow.

Questions for a Review Process

Questions to ask and what to do with the

answers when starting a peer review process.

"Every development process is different." Maybe, but successful peer review deployments do have common elements. No matter how you tailor your process, you should be aware of the typical issues and pitfalls so you're making informed decisions.

What are the goals of review?

The answer might seem obvious, but it is perhaps the most important question to answer, and it must be answered in a certain way.

There are many possible benefits of code review. You'll find more defects in development. Your code will be well-documented. You'll be able to mentor and direct new hires while allowing them to jump into the code quickly.

No matter what your primary goals are, some of these effects will happen. But if you're not able to define and measure a specific goal you won't be able to judge whether peer review is really achieving the results you require.

For one of our customers, the goal was to reduce support costs. In particular, it cost them $33 per customer support call, and the company wanted to reduce the number of calls per year from 50,000. Code review was used both to remove defects (incorrect behavior or errant error dialogs would generate calls) and to improve usability (if you can't figure out how to do something, you call support). Over a few years the support calls were down to 20,000 even with a 2-fold increase in product sales, representing $2.6 million in savings[1].

For another customer, the goal was to reduce the number of defects introduced during development. The metrics group had a phase-injection chart[2], and the numbers for development didn't look good. Most of the defects found by QA were caused by faulty code, not a result of bad design or incorrect requirements. And development's numbers were even worse for defects found by end users. The goal of code review was simple: To reduce the number of defects injected by development. Fortunately, with a good metrics process already in place and using a tool-assisted code review process that tracked defect metrics automatically, it was easy for them to directly measure their progress and to attempt various review techniques until they found a process that uncovered the majority of the defects while minimizing time spent

---

[1] With doubled sales, the expected number of support calls is 100,000. The savings is the cost of the 80,000 calls that never occurred.

[2] A phase-injection chart is a tool that shows (a) in which development phase each defect was "injected" (introduced) and (b) in which development phase each defect was found. The chart can answer questions like "How effective is QA at finding defects before customers do?" and "How often are incorrect requirements at fault rather than developer error" and "How many errors are caused by faulty code rather than bad design?" See the first essay in this collection for an example.

performing the reviews. Code review eliminated defects released from development to QA, just as design and architecture meetings eliminate defects released from design to development.

The thing to notice is that in both cases the answer to the question "What is the goal of the review" was a directly measurable quantity, not an ambiguous statement like "fix more bugs." You must have a quantifiable measure of success or else you cannot know if your review process is making a difference. "Number of support calls per month" or "Percent of defects injected by development" are measurable values.

In many cases having a measurable goal also means you can assign a dollar value to achieving the goal. This can be useful when convincing the powers-at-be that installing a review process makes business sense. Even without a monetary value, just having a measurable goal makes it easier to pitch the idea because you're holding yourself accountable. If it doesn't work out, everyone will see that, and you'll try something else.

It also helps when you're ready to tweak the process. You'll want to change the checklists, change how often you perform reviews, change which code you require to have reviews, change how much time you spend reviewing, and so on. Which changes make things better? Or worse? Only if the results are measurable can you answer these questions with confidence.

The goal doesn't have to be complicated. For example, if your general goal is to fix more defects, make an informal scan of the last several hundred bugs and determine how many of them you believe should have been prevented had you had a code review process in place. Then you can make a goal such as "Reduce number of reported defects by 50%" or "Fix at least as many defects in code review as are reported by QA and customers together."

How amenable are your developers to review?

We see two distinct reactions when management announces a new code review policy. In some groups they realize their defects are out of control, they're scared to make code changes, or they know some new group is making worrisome changes willy-nilly in their code base. These groups want review because they know it will address their existing complaints.

The other (more common) reaction is negative. "Oh great, more process." "Now I'll have to do more work just to check something in to ClearCase." "I wonder if we'll be fired if our code has too many defects." This is typical with developers who have never done code review or who have had irresponsible managers in the past.

In this case you have several options. The "baby-steps" approach starts with something easy to swallow. For example, give everyone the tools for code review, but don't require reviews. Just suggest that whenever a developer believes a review is warranted, get someone else to review it. Use your judgment and don't worry about metrics. Just use this as another tool to help keep the code base solid. New hires should use this much more often to double-check that they didn't break anything unknowingly.

Once the group gets used to the idea of review, they'll also start seeing some of the positive social and personal aspects of review[3], and they'll see that it does contribute positively to the development process. Then you can start enforcing review in certain cases – all changes on a stable branch, or in a certain code module, or when the change is particularly complex. It's easy to get developers on board with that idea once they agree that code review is helpful in the first place.

Another baby-step is to have "random drug test" reviews. Just take version control check-ins at random and review them.

---

[3] When done correctly, code review can be personally rewarding and fun. See "Social Aspects of Review" elsewhere in this essay collection.

One advantage of this is that you can control exactly how much time is spent performing reviews. Another is that you'll get higher code quality across the board because of the Ego Effect[4].

Eventually you can roll out review on a wide basis. Depending on the goals of review, you might not need to review every single code change; use your measurement of success to impose just enough review to achieve the goal.

How will you improve the process over time?

There are many reasons why the peer review process is dynamic. No process is perfect when it first rolls out. Software development changes over the lifetime of the project. Development techniques change over time.

It's not a question of whether the process will change; it's a question of how you will know what needs changing and how you will measure the effect of your changes.

To measure any process you need metrics. In the case of code review there are two kinds: external metrics that measure the overall effectiveness of the process and internal metrics that measure rates and values coming from the act of review.

The external metrics are those wrapped up in your definition of the goal of the review. In our earlier examples these were "number of monthly support requests" or "percentage of defects injected by development." These are the ultimate measure of the success of the code review program, and these are the numbers to watch over time. If your initial results are good but you start slipping, this is indicates the process needs changing; after a change, an improvement in these metrics are the final proof that the change was successful.

---

[4] The "Ego Effect" is that just knowing that someone else might look at your code is enough to get developers to self-check their work and generally be more careful. It is fully described in the "Social Aspects of Review" essay elsewhere in this collection.

Although ultimately the external metrics are all that matter, frequently the feedback is slow and blind. For example, to determine whether a new process affected the number of support calls, you have to wait until the new version is released, then wait for customers to get their hands on it, then wait for enough calls to start coming in to see if there was any effect. Meanwhile many months have passed, and in the interim you have zero feedback.

This is where the internal metrics come in. The most common of these are:

- Inspection Rate. "How fast are we able to review code?" Normally measured in kLOC/man-hour.
- Defect Rate. "How fast are we able to find defects?" Normally measured in defects/man-hour.
- Defect Density. "How many defects do we expect to find in a given amount of code?" Normally measured in defects/kLOC.

The exact values of these measures depend on many factors including the type of development (new code, maintenance), stability of the code (final, beta, development), complexity of the changes, experience of the developers and reviewers, programming tools and languages, and amount of time spent in review. As with any metric, the important thing is to compare apples with apples – as you watch the process change over time, compare changes of similar complexity in similar code modules within the same development groups.

As you change the process, watch these numbers. Decide ahead of time what you'd expect to happen. For example, say you decide you need to do a better job keeping defects out of the stable code branch. So you change the process with the intention of having more reviewers look at any stable branch changes. You expect the inspection rate to drop (because more people are spending more time on every change) and you expect the defect density to increase (because for a given change you're wanting more defects to be uncovered). These are values you can measure quickly – over the space of even just ten reviews or a few weeks.

Although the external metrics are the only true indicator of the success of a change to the process, internal metrics give you fast feedback on how well you're achieving the more immediate goals.

There are several other essays in this collection that describe the types of metrics you can collect, what those metrics mean, what they don't mean, what other development groups have done with them, and what the published literature tells us.

How will you collect metrics?

Developers hate collecting metrics. And for good reason: no one wants to do a code review holding a stopwatch and wielding line-counting tools.

Even if you try to mandate such things, people forget to do it. In studies with our customers as well as in observing our own development process, we found that "stop-watch" style measurement is extremely inaccurate. During a review there might be in interruption – a phone call, an e-mail, or even a bathroom break. Frequently you forget to pause the timer. When you get back, sometimes you forget to account for the missing time, and even when you do it's often a guess.

And it gets worse! Our field experience is that developers often just make up numbers that they believe make them look good. The irony is that often the developer doesn't change the metric to his favor because he incorrectly assumes what a "good" value is. For example, the most common cheat is to report less time-in-review than was actually spent. The developer believes this is good because it shows he is more efficient at finding defects. But studies have repeatedly shown that only by spending *more* time in review will you find more defects! Another common cheat goes the other way – to report more time spent on review than actually took place to appear as though the review has happened when in fact the developer is shirking his responsibility. Again, the mismatch between defect density and time-on-task exposes the cheat.

Only an automated or tightly controlled process can give you repeatable metrics. Clearly line-counting tools should be used for lines-changed and lines-inspected measurements.

Automated timing systems have to be intelligent to be effective. Just putting "start" and "stop" buttons in a computer interface does not solve the stopwatch problem. It might get your numbers into a database, but you still have the problems of dealing with interruptions or with off-line activity (e.g. whiteboard discussions).

Your timing system needs to be smart enough to account for these external factors. Being inaccurate even by 15 minutes can throw off your rate metrics by an order of magnitude[5].

How will you manage negative emotions?

Criticism is personal. No matter how thick-skinned you are, when you put out your best effort and someone else finds fault, it's not a nice feeling. Some people can put away those feelings and accept the process as being good for the project as well as an opportunity for personal improvement, but inevitably there will be strife.

Another different problem arises with any process that involves collecting metrics or audit trails. Developers, through misconceptions or experiences with unreasonable managers, often feel like "Big Brother" is watching. The biggest concern is

---

[5] Blatant Plug: At Smart Bear we performed empirical tests (with stopwatches at customer sites) to see if activity logs in our web-based code review tool could be used to predict "actual time on task" even including external factors. We developed a heuristic that correlated very well with reality. The result is we can compute "man-hours on task" without any human input (no start/stop buttons) accurately enough for metrics analysis. This is a part of our Code Collaborator product described elsewhere in this essay collection.

whether code review metrics will impact their performance evaluations.

At the very least there are specific things managers can do in development meetings to mitigate these feelings. We've devoted a whole essay to the subject.

Some groups take this one step further and have professional training sessions with their developers and reviewers. Everyone can learn how to accept criticism without taking it personally, and reviewers can learn techniques and language that lessens these feelings. Unfortunately, our experience is that even professional training cannot overcome the illogic of human emotion, so the techniques given in the "Social Aspects" chapter should still be employed.

How will you develop the review checklist?

The checklist is an important component of any review. There are several ways to build a checklist; you'll want to determine which technique is most appropriate for your development group.

Checklists are most effective at detecting omissions. Omissions are typically the most difficult types of errors to find. After all, you don't need a checklist to tell a reviewer to look for algorithm errors or sensible documentation – that's what a reviewer will naturally do when confronted with source code. The difficult thing is to notice when something is *not* there. For example, the checklist can remind the reviewer to confirm that all errors are handled, that function arguments are tested for invalid values, and that unit tests have been created. If the author forgot it, the reviewer is likely to forget it as well.

In fact, as long as the reviewer has a checklist, shouldn't the author have it as well? Why shouldn't the author get the same reminders? Of course authors should, which is why checklists should be stored in easy-to-access places such as shared drives or an intranet or even checked into version control along with the source code. This doesn't relieve the reviewer of his duties but it does help the author get his changes through review on the first pass.

In a more extreme case of this, the PSP[6] suggests that each author should have his own personal checklist. The SEI points out that each person make 15-20 common mistakes; if you notice what they are (through peer review) you can develop your own personal checklist. Authors can even give their personal checklist to reviewers.

The content of the checklist will depend on the purpose of the review. A security audit will have items such as "All input data is cleansed before use" and "All invalid input data is rejected." A style review will contain items such as "All methods are documented according to company standards" or "All private member fields start with an underscore."

We are frequently asked for examples of items that make sense on a checklist. The following is a guide that should get you thinking about the various categories of items that might appear on the checklist. Keep in mind that the longer the checklist gets the less effective each item is, so try to keep it down to the 10-20 items that you find most often wrong.

Sample Checklist Items

1. Documentation: All subroutines are commented in clear language.

2. Documentation: Describe what happens with corner-case input.

3. Documentation: Complex algorithms are explained and justified.

---

6 The PSP (Personal Software Process) and SEI (Software Engineering Institute) with their policies on code review and checklists is fully described in its own essay in this collection.

4. Documentation: Code that depends on non-obvious behavior in external libraries is documented with reference to external documentation.

5. Documentation: Units of measurement are documented for numeric values.

6. Documentation: Incomplete code is indicated with appropriate distinctive markers (e.g. "TODO" or "FIXME").

7. Documentation: User-facing documentation is updated (on-line help, contextual help, tool-tips, version history).

8. Testing: Unit tests are added for new code paths or behaviors.

9. Testing: Unit tests cover errors and invalid parameter cases.

10. Testing: Unit tests demonstrate the algorithm is performing as documented.

11. Testing: Possible null pointers always checked before use.

12. Testing: Array indexes checked to avoid out-of-bound errors.

13. Testing: Don't write new code that is already implemented in an existing, tested API.

14. Testing: New code fixes/implements the issue in question.

15. Error Handling: Invalid parameter values are handled properly early in the subroutine.

16. Error Handling: Error values of null pointers from subroutine invocations are checked.

17. Error Handling: Error handlers clean up state and resources no matter where an error occurs.

18. Error Handling: Memory is released, resources are closed, and reference counters are managed under both error and non-error conditions.

19. Thread Safety: Global variables are protected by locks or locking subroutines.

20. Thread Safety: Objects accessed by multiple threads are accessed only through a lock.

21. Thread Safety: Locks must be acquired and released in the right order to prevent deadlocks, even in error-handling code.

22. Performance: Objects are duplicated only when necessary.

23. Performance: No busy-wait loops instead of proper thread-synchronization methods.

24. Performance: Memory usage is acceptable even with large inputs.

25. Performance: Optimization that makes code harder to read should only be implemented if a profiler or other tool has indicated that the routine stands to gain from optimization. These kinds of optimizations should be well-documented and code that performs the same task simply should be preserved somewhere.

The most effective way to build and maintain your checklist is to match defects found during review to the associated checklist item (if any). Items that turn up many defects should be kept. Defects that aren't associated with any checklist item should be scanned periodically. Usually there are categorical trends in your defects; turn each type of defect into a checklist item that would cause the reviewer to find it.

Over time your team will become used to the more common checklist items and will adopt programming habits that prevent some of them altogether. You can accelerate and codify this by reviewing the "Top 5 Most Violated" checklist items every month to determine whether anything can be done to help developers avoid the problem. For example, if a common problem is "not all methods are fully documented," you might be able to enable a feature in your IDE that requires developers to have at least some sort of documentation on every method.

Stay vigilant

The common theme to all these suggestions is to keep an eye on things. Of course your first attempt at code review won't be perfect, but with a few measurements and occasional process review you can tune your methods over time. And even the best process shouldn't stagnate as the needs of the development group change.

Make a conscientious effort to pay attention to how things are going, keep the dialog open with everyone involved, and keep your eye on your clearly-stated goal for success.

Measurement & Improvement

Which metrics are useful, what do they mean,

what do they not mean, and how to use them

to improve the process.

You can't fix what you can't measure. Before you can understand your code review process – much less take action to change it – you need objective measurements. Metrics can tell you how efficient your reviews are, whether you are saving money compared to other methods of defect removal, help you predict how many hours you'll need to complete a project, and measure the impact of a change to the process.

Raw measurements

What about your review process is worth measuring? Before you get into analysis, what are the raw numbers you should be collecting?

LOC

You can always measure the number of lines of code (LOC) under review. If you're reviewing documents instead of source code, this is often in "pages" or "lines" (typically 30-40 lines per page). This is the basic unit of "size" of the review.

Some pundits suggest using non-whitespace lines of code instead of total lines of code. The idea is that extra whitespace probably doesn't affect the true "size" of the review or the complexity of the task at hand. Others go further and suggest counting the number of lines of source code ignoring whitespace (often abbreviated sLOC).

Although we agree that sLOC is better correlated with "executable code" than is LOC, in our experience the comments often have as much to do with the review as the source code. Many defects are found in document/code mismatch or just in lack of proper documentation. Therefore we believe LOC is a better measure of the amount of work necessary for the reviewer.

Inspection Time

Inspection time is simply the amount of time reviewers spend looking for defects. It is typically measured in hours and 6-minute accuracy is generally considered to be very good.

Although easy to define, inspection time can be quite difficult to measure accurately. The most obvious technique is to have reviewers use a stopwatch to time themselves. The problems with this are many: you forget to start the stopwatch, it's hard to account for interruptions, and developers just don't like having to do it.

One way to address the difficulty in collecting accurate numbers is to use a tool-assisted review process where software presents the code material (and logs defects and conversations). Such software can often determine the amount of time in the review automatically making developers happy and recording repeatable metrics.

Defect Count

A "defect" is something a reviewer wants changed in the code. It could be as serious as a bug in an algorithm or as trivial as some reformatting or typo in a comment.

The defect count is perhaps the most important metric because it indicates how much effect the review is having. If reviews are not coming up with defects, something is wrong. The only way to measure the effectiveness of reviewing (as opposed to unit tests, QA, beta, etc.) is by comparing the number of defects uncovered by each.

With formal inspections or tool-assisted reviews, counting defects is typically trivial because you have official defect logs. If you're reviewing over-the-shoulder or by email, it can be difficult to get a proper defect count.

Analytical metrics

These three raw values are the measurements you can make directly on your review process but they don't help you make decisions or comparative analysis.

From certain ratios of these raw values we approach more useful data. Typically these ratios are taken across many reviews in a group – all the reviews of a certain author, or performed by a certain reviewer, or by a development group, or on a set of files.

Inspection Rate

The inspection rate is the speed at which a certain amount of code is reviewed. The ratio is LOC divided by inspection hours. An expected value for a meticulous inspection would be 100-200 LOC/hour; a normal inspection might be 200-500. Above 800-1000 is so fast that you can probably conclude the review did a perfunctory job.

Defect Rate

The defect rate is the speed at which defects are uncovered by reviewers. The ratio is defect count divided by inspection hours.

A typical value for source code would be 5-20 defects per hour depending on the review technique. For example, formal inspections with both private code-reading phases and inspection meetings will be on the slow end, whereas the lightweight approaches – especially those without scheduled inspection meetings – will be on the high end.

Note that this counts only the time spent uncovering the defects in review, not the time it takes to actually fix those defects.

Defect Density

The defect density is the number of defects found in a given amount of source code. The ratio is defect count divided by kLOC (thousand lines of code). The higher the defect density, the more defects you are uncovering which usually means the review is being more effective. That is, a high defect density is more likely to mean the reviewers did a great job than it is to mean the underlying source code is extremely bad.

It is impossible to give one expected value for defect density. A mature, stable code base with tight development controls might have a defect density as low as 5 defects/kLOC; new code written by junior developers in an uncontrolled environment but where the review process is strict might uncover 100-200 defects/kLOC.

Analysis: What the metrics really tell us

The most natural question is: What are "good" values for these metrics? And the follow-up: If our metrics are "bad," what can we do to correct the problem?

It's tempting to assign "good" and "bad" values for rates and defect density. To illustrate the difficulties with this evaluation, consider these two examples.

Example A: Source code is located in a stable branch and is part of a critical back-end module. 70% of the application depends on the behavior in this module. The author makes changes to only a few lines of source code, but because of the risk of bug-injection the team decides to assign three reviewers to look for problems. The reviewers, knowing the consequence of any defect, spend a lot of time pouring over the few changes, following program flow into many other files to check that the change won't inject a bug elsewhere, making sure documentation is especially verbose, and considering many possible use-case scenarios for the logic being altered.

In the end, the reviewers find five defects and the three reviewers spend six collective hours on the task.

Example B: Source code is located in a development branch. The author has implemented a change to a new GUI dialog box involving a new interactive element. Some of the code was generated by the GUI-builder tool. In total 120 lines of code were added or modified. One reviewer is assigned to this change. He can't make much sense out of the generated code (e.g. is "243,134" the correct coordinates for the top-left corner of the element?), so he speeds through that and takes more time with the code backing the GUI element.

In the end, the reviewer finds one defect and spends thirty minutes on the task.

Now consider the metrics that would fall out of these two examples. Example A has a high defect density (4 defects in a few lines), a slow code inspection rate (6 hours for a few lines), and a defect rate of about 1 defect per hour. Example B has a low defect density (1 defect in 120 lines), a fast code inspection rate (120 lines in 30 minutes), and a defect rate of 2 defects per hour.

These metrics are quite different. Was it bad that Example A had a high defect density? Should that developer be chastised for introducing so many bugs in so little space? Probably not – in this case the high density is the result of reviewers nit-picking at every possible thing. In fact, the high defect density is probably a good sign – an indication that the reviewers were thorough and we can be relatively confident in the quality of the code after the change.

Conversely, should the reviewer in Example B be chastised for a low defect density? After all, a low density might mean the reviewer didn't do his job! Probably not – it's difficult for anyone to review generated code (especially when QA can readily and efficiently find defects in the dialog), and because the rest of the code is under active development, we intentionally didn't have the reviewer spend so much time investigating problems.

So much for defect density. The same type of arguments can be made for the other metrics. In Example A we see very slow inspection rates; case studies have shown that the slower the rate the more confident you can be in removing defects, so this is a good sign[1]. On the other hand, it would be bad if the reviewer in Example B spent the same amount of time per line of code – he would have been in inspection for weeks!

Interestingly, in these examples the rate of defects per hour is not very different (compared to the other values which are vastly different). This makes sense because you'd expect that if someone is staring at code, whether scanning quickly or being very careful, he will uncover problems only as fast as he can process the information. Indeed, this is another indication that for code where you'd expect to find more defects (complex code) or want to fix more defects (risky code) you will want reviewers to spend more time looking at it – and also expect them to actually find more defects, even if they are more trivial than usual.

So the first point of these examples is: *Defect rates for a reviewer are task-independent.* Knowing this, you should assign reviewer-time based on the complexity of risk of the task. You cannot expect

---

[1] An oft-cited result with formal inspections in "mission-critical" projects (e.g. pacemakers, fly-by-wire, NASA) is "one hour per page," where "page" means a printed page of source code or design document. Shockingly slow, perhaps – with non-mission-critical you can relax this rate – but repeatedly we see increased defect densities as rates approach this limit. A detailed treatment of this effect can be found in several other essays in this collection.

reviewers to find more defects in a given amount of time just because the code is more complex.

The second point of these examples is: *The meaning of metrics depends on the goal of the review.* In reviews of critical or complex code we naturally expect greater defect densities and slower inspection rates; in reviews of simple code, confusing generated code, or code that is changing rapidly, we expect the opposite. For security audits we might expect yet other metrics.

You might have noticed that we've mostly avoided guidelines on what these numbers "ought" to be. If the case studies have taught us anything it's that every development group is different – even groups within a single business unit. The repeated recommendation is to start collecting metrics and revisit them regularly[2] to see what the trends are and see which numbers are out of expected range.

You must be careful to split out defect metrics by code modules, reviewers, and possibly severities and types. As these two examples illustrate, the location of the code and severity of the defect changes the numbers completely; meaning is lost if you average all metrics together across all reviews.

Comparative analysis

Another interesting analysis can be made if you have similar metrics from QA. Let's say you know that a "major" severity defect in the GUI takes an average of 10 hours to find in QA, fix in development, and verify in QA. You can get the same metrics for those types of defects in code review. By comparing the two, you can determine how to fix the most defects in the least amount of time.

For example, null-pointer exception problems are usually very easy to spot in peer review. The reviewer points out the line of

---

[2] Once a month, or once per "iteration" in the software development lifecycle.

code where the problem is. The fix is usually one or two lines of code, and again is usually easy and obvious. The validation is similarly fast. On the other hand, in QA these problems usually manifest themselves as an error dialog that often presents a message that obscures the underlying problem (e.g. "Sorry, the file couldn't be written.") The developer has to reproduce the problem and hunt down the location of the problem.

For GUI code – especially generated code – the opposite is true. It's easy for QA to identify something like "this button is not aligned with the rest" and also easy for the developer to fix in the GUI-builder, but this would be impractical for a code reviewer to detect.

In these examples it's obvious which types of issues are more efficient in code review and which in QA, but others are not so obvious. With a rigorous, matching metrics process on both sides, you can measure this difference and change the process accordingly. Process change might mean changing your review changelist (e.g. "Don't review GUI code") or self-training on how to become more efficient at detecting some specific class of error.

Of course this type of comparative analysis shouldn't be limited to QA. You should also record defects found in alpha- and beta-testing and by customers in the field. The most comprehensive approach to this type of comparative analysis is called "phase-injection" analysis.

Measuring the effectiveness of review: Phase-Injection

When a customer reports a defect, is it because our requirements were wrong? Or because we didn't design correctly? Or because of a bug in the software implementation? Or a configuration file created by QA?

These questions are important because if you want to eliminate defects you have to first know what part of your development organization is responsible for creating those defects. This isn't about placing blame on individuals; it's about understanding which part of the process needs adjusting.

For example, if most customer issues arise from a misunderstanding of how the product works, this means we need more work in requirements. Perhaps we could conduct usability studies to empirically determine requirements; after all, users are notoriously good at criticism but bad at coming up with hard requirements.

This analysis is usually plotted on a "phase-injection" chart. The chart in Figure 25 is taken from one of our customers who decided to collect this data for a small development project.

		Bug injected in this phase				
		Req's	Design	Devmnt	QA/Test	Cost*
Phase Discovered	Req's	0				$0
	Design	3	0			$45
	Devmnt	8	3	0		$275
	QA/Test	21	2	142	0	$33,000
	Customer	14	0	127	0	$141,000
	Totals:	46	5	269	0	$174,320

Figure 25: Phase-Injection chart. The phase that caused the defect is plotted vertically; the phase where the defect was found is plotted horizontally.

*Cost-to-fix was estimated with data from IBM Israel. See later footnote text for details.

This chart plots all defects registered with the issue-tracker for this project. The column is determined by the development phase in which the bug was introduced into the product; the row is determined by the phase in which the bug was caught (that is, entered into the issue-tracker). Data on where the bug was caught is easy to come by – just use the date on the issue. The trick is in knowing the phase injected. This can be determined in a post-mortem analysis of the issues or, as in their case, by adding a field for "phase injected" in the issue-tracker itself.

There are three interesting things to notice on this chart. First, the diagonal contains only zeros. This is because defects found inside a phase are generally corrected on the spot and not recorded separately in the issue tracker. For example, if a design problem is found in a design meeting, you don't open an issue, correct the design, and close the issue; you just correct the design.

The second thing to notice is the disproportionately large number of defects injected by development. Finding these defects takes the bulk of QA resources and causes the bulk of the customer complaints. Some people find this result "obvious" since software implementation not only represents the largest effort (in man-hours) but is also the most detail-oriented.

The third important aspect is the total cost of these defects. Of course defects found by customers are the most expensive; clearly the large quantity of bugs created in the development phase is also to blame here. The exact dollar amounts are not as important as the relative amounts[3]; the point is the later in the development process a defect is found the more expensive it is to fix.

---

[3] Everyone agrees that defects found by customers are many times as expensive to fix as those found in beta, which are more than found in testing, which are more than unit testing, etc.. Exact numbers are hard to find because you want to include things like "consumer ill-will" which has definite value but is difficult to quantify. The numbers in this chart came from IBM and are useful as a guide. A study at Hewlett-Packard showed much higher costs with customer-found defects 100x the cost of those found during review.

If we want fewer issues reported, we have to stop development from releasing so many defects to QA. This is where code review comes in.

So what happened when this development group employed code review on the next project? Actually an even better question is: What would have happened had they used code review on this project?

Fortunately we know the answer to that question! Because the goal of this project was to investigate the effect of code review on their development environment, they implemented a code review process retroactively on each of their source code changes. Because the developers and testers involved already knew about these errors, a different group of people did the code review and subsequent testing.

As for the customer issues, they assumed the customer reports would be the same, but of course they eliminated the report of any issue that was fixed during this second run-through. This was the one part of the experiment that couldn't be re-done properly.

Figure 26 shows the result. Again there are several things to notice.

First, the total number of defects is greater than without code review! Does this mean that code review introduced more defects in the code than there was before? No, it means that more defects were uncovered with code review than without. The code at the end of the review process was better[4] than it had been before.

---

[4] Developers involved in the study reported not only more "bugs" fixed but also code that was better documented due to defects like "I don't understand what this code does."

	Phase Injected				
	Req's	Design	Devmnt	QA/Test	Cost*
Req's	0				$0
Design	3	0			$45
Devmnt	8	11	283		$7,550
QA/Test	21	0	67	0	$17,600
Customer	14	0	81	0	$95,000
Totals:	46	11	431	0	$120,195

Figure 26: The same phase-injection chart with code review applied.

Second, the number of design-related bugs doubled. Again, code review uncovered problems with design that weren't caught before. This makes sense – if you're examining your code and talking about potential problems with organization and scalability, you might stumble across some issues that you didn't think about during design. So after review the developers also had a better idea of what was wrong with the design – useful information for the next iteration.

Third, the total cost of defects went down 30%. This result is impressive when you consider that the total number of defects increased by 60%. We were able to remove many more defects so cheaply that the overall cost went down! Again, the exact dollar amount is not important. The point is that we moved defects from more expensive to less expensive phases.

Code review made every aspect of the project more successful – more defects removed, code more maintainable, fewer customer complaints, and lower total cost of defects.

The SEI Perspective

The science of code reviews from the perspective

of the SEI, PSP, TSP, and CMMI.

"Your PSP reviews will net you a greater return
than any other single thing you can do."
—Watts Humphrey

Written by Steven Teleki.

The software process models from the Software Engineering Institute (SEI)[1]: the Personal Software Process (PSP), Team Software Process (TSP), and Capability Maturity Model Integration (CMMI) consider reviews to be an integral part of a software process capable of producing high quality results on an optimal

---

[1] CMM, CMMI, and Capability Maturity Model are registered in the U.S. Patent and Trademark Office by Carnegie Mellon University. PSP, Personal Software Process, TSP, Team Software Process are service marks of Carnegie Mellon University.

schedule. Reviews in the PSP and TSP are checklist-driven personal reviews with a 70% to 90% yield. The return on investment (ROI) of the reviews is measured and actively improved. Software engineers performing personal reviews see their performance, skills, and knowledge continually improve because of the timely feedback that the process provides.

About the PSP, TSP and CMMI

The Capability Maturity Model (CMM) is the precursor of the three process models. It was published in a 1989 book by Watts Humphrey called *Managing the Software Process*. About a decade later, the CMM evolved into the CMMI or Capability Maturity Model Integration.

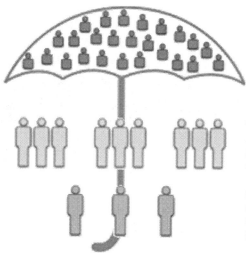

Capability Maturity Model Integration (CMMI): Focuses on the organization's capability; management actions.

Team Software Process (TSP): Focuses on team performance; product development.

Personal Software Process (PSP): Focuses on individual skills and discipline; entirely personal.

Figure 27: The TSP builds on PSP, and CMMI keeps it all together.

The CMMI is a five level process model that groups capabilities that a software organization can successfully perfect. Each level builds on top of the previous level. Achieving Level 5 means that an organization has successfully implemented a feedback loop that enables it to continually improve its processes.

As the SEI worked with organizations using CMM-based process models, they realized that the success of the organizational improvement hinges on the individual engineer. The PSP came out of the SEI's desire to assist the individual engineer in effective improvement based on his or her own personal process data. The PSP was originally published in Humphrey's book called *A Discipline for Software Engineering* in 1995. The PSP assists at the very personal level, where the engineer is alone with the computer. At this level the process is one's own responsibility.

The TSP builds on highly capable individuals and adds product development related process elements. It came about because the engineers using the PSP needed a method to effectively use the rich set of personal data for the benefit of the software team.

Personal Background

Back in 1992 when I needed process help on a small software project I picked up *Managing the Software Process*. It turns out that I could use many of Humphrey's ideas *on a small scale*. By the time he published *A Discipline for Software Engineering*, the book where he introduced the PSP in 1995, I was ready for it.

In 1999 I participated in one of the very first TSP pilot projects and worked on refining the TSP for projects with hard deadlines and millions of end-users.

The personal software process has been the most appealing of all the software process improvement initiatives that I am familiar with. The reason is that the PSP is a direct process between software engineer and machine. At this level, all processes are personal. What gets written and how it is written is up to me. More so, if something goes wrong, there is nobody else to blame. If the process doesn't work, then it is up to me to change it, fix it, and make it work.

Since 1999 I taught the PSP class to over 120 engineers, managers, and executives. Universally, the biggest hurdle has been learning and practicing the concepts. But once the habits were built, the engineers have been able to successfully use them to improve their performance and their working lives.

Reviews in the PSP

Reviews in the PSP are checklist-driven personal reviews. The review process is measured by the individual engineer, analyzed, and improved using the data collected.

<u>Checklist Driven Reviews</u>

Every software process consists of one or more phases. The most common software process in use today consists of two phases: Code and Test.

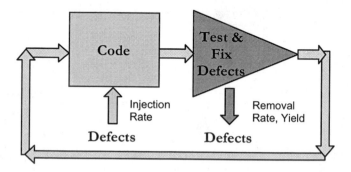

Figure 28: Code 'n Test Software Process

During the Code phase the developer writes the software code, and during the Test phase the developer runs the program, finds the defects and fixes them, then proceeds to do more coding and more testing.

The Code phase has an associated Defect Injection Rate. If it didn't, then there would be no need to do the Test phase. However, this is not the case. In every human activity, we are bound to make some mistakes, and coding is no exception. The number of defects that we inject into the product is a factor of our knowledge: our knowledge of the tools we use, the domain in which we operate, and the activity that we perform.

The purpose of the Test phase then is to remove the defects from the product. It has an associated Defect Removal Rate and Yield. The defect removal rate of the Test phase tends to be low relative to the removal rate of other phases. Therefore, to cut the schedule, we introduce a Code Review phase with a removal rate that is at least double that of the Test phase. The yield of the Code Review phase is also 50 to 80% better than that of the Test phase.

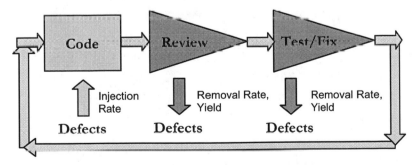

Figure 29: Software Process including a Code Review

Beyond "The Hammer"

If all you have is a hammer, everything looks like a nail. —*proverb*
As you look back at Figure 29 you cannot help but wonder about
the nature of the defects removed by the Code Review and Test
phases. They must all be coding defects since that was the only
phase performed. We all know that this scenario is highly unlikely.
There is a good chance that some of the defects are architecture
defects, some are requirements defects and some are design
defects.

Software development work consists of a variety of activities.
If you clearly delineate the phases then you are able to properly
understand where your skills are sufficient to perform high quality
work and where you are lacking skills or knowledge to excel. This
means that at the individual level you need to outline in your
process the phases in which you are performing architecture,
design, or coding tasks. This and a definition of when those
phases are complete allow you to properly identify the source of
your defects.

When you define the phases of your work, in essence you are
setting up your very own "information supply chain." In this
supply chain you have phases that generate a work product and
you have phases that remove defects from the previously created
work product. An example is Code phase followed by Code
Review phase. Another example would be a Design phase
followed by Design Review phase. The generative phases create
work products that feed the following generative phase, like the
Design phase feeds the Code phase.

Your "Defects"

What are your defects? A defect is an error in the program. This
error is there because of a mistake that you made. Don't get too
defensive: we all make mistakes. The key point is that you recog-
nize that you might make mistakes and that you devise cheap ways
to get them out of your program. Enter "your review checklist."

A Review Checklist

A review checklist contains statements that help you look for mistakes that you made in the past. These statements are true/false statements. They leave no wiggle room. They are not open-ended.

Each statement is written to check for a class of defects, not just a single instance of a defect. The statements are the result of the defect analysis that you perform periodically to see how well the checklist is working for you.

Checklist Items for C++ Programming	True/False
Dynamically allocated memory is freed by the same module that allocated it.	

Figure 30: Sample Code Review Checklist Item for C++

The checklist item from Figure 30 used to be on my personal code review checklist for a while. Once I successfully adopted this programming idiom I prevented memory leaks in my programs.

Performing a Checklist-Driven Review

To perform the checklist-driven review you take your checklist and for each checklist item you review the entire work product that is the subject of your review. This is very important point. There is evidence that reviews are much more effective when you look for one checklist item at a time in the entire work product. When you put a checkmark by the statement, you are certifying that the work product is free of this defect. This is tougher than it sounds, but at the same time is also very liberating. You will start deeply trusting your work. You won't be just "guessing" that the code might work, you'll know it.

Treat each checkmark on your checklist as a *personal quality certificate* that the work product is free of this defect.

When you notice a defect, you then record the defect and continue with the review of the work product for the same checklist item. Keep your mind focused on finding the defects, not on fixing them. You are much more effective when you clearly separate these activities.

As you are looking for the defects based on your checklist items, you will be finding other defects that are not yet captured by your checklist items. Record them as well and mark them as "new" since you'll have to analyze them later and create checklist items based on them. Occasionally you'll find a new defect that you suspect might occur in the rest of the work products that you already checked. Then you will have to go back and recheck them.

After you have reviewed all work products for all checklist items, you proceed to fix the defects that you recorded. Fixing the defects found in code review is easier then fixing the defects found in testing. The reason is that when you find a defect in code review you are looking at the source of defect, while when you are fixing a defect in testing, first you have to figure out the source of the defect, since in testing you only get the symptom of the defect.

Getting Started with Checklist-Driven Reviews

You create a checklist from the defects that you find in your work. As you work on software development projects, you record defect data. A defect is anything that is wrong with the software once a particular phase is over. This highlights once more the importance of defining phases in your personal software process.

When you decide to perform checklist-driven reviews, you will not have any defect data, since you were not yet in the habit of recording your defects. You may have some system test defects.

You have to think back to the last few defects that you can recall and build a checklist from those 3 to 5 defects that you remember. Analyze these defects. Assign a class to each defect. Chances are that not each defect will be in a class by itself. You'll have several defects that can be traced back to the same root cause.

Once you are in the habit of recording your defects, then at the end of each iteration (which is usually every few days or every week), you analyze the defect data, identify the classes of defects that occurred, and write the appropriate checklist statements that attempt to prevent an entire class of defects. The outcome of the defect analysis is that the defects are categorized, and each category receives one statement for the defect review checklist.

When it comes to recording defect data you have to be honest with yourself. After all, this is all data that you are recording for yourself. There is no point in trying to make up your data. Your goal should be to develop a deep understanding of how you work, and how you think about your software development work.

Frequently Asked Questions about Personal Reviews

Q: Why would I want to review? It is slow and my testing catches defects quicker.

A: Do not listen to me or to anybody else about the effectiveness of the reviews. Just give it a try. See if it works for you. Keep in mind that in a review you'll be staring directly at the defect, as opposed to the symptom of a defect like you do in testing.

There were folks with 20+ years of software development experience who told me that they don't see the need to do reviews. Until they tried it for a few times, that is. Right in one of the first reviews they conducted, they usually would find a defect that according to their own estimate would've caused them hours of testing and fixing time, but in review they caught it and fixed it in minutes.

Q: OK, I want to get started. Where to do I get my first checklist from?

A: This question comes up because often developers feel that if they don't have a *complete* list, then they might as well not have any at all. However, this need not be the case. You can build your first checklist out of those 2-3 items that you recall that caused a defect most recently. If you keep recording your defects, soon you'll have a checklist that's just about right for you.

Q: I make so many defects that my checklist will be very long and it will not be practical for me to check my code for each of those defects. What should I do?

A: An interesting paradox will happen. As soon as you start recording your defects you will start making fewer defects. This may seem odd to you. But I, and many other folks using or coaching the PSP, have seen it happen over and over. A personal defect review checklist settles at about half page in size, or about 15-20 items at most. Maybe it is surprising to you, but you tend to make the same mistakes over and over, for a while anyway. When you learn how to prevent a certain mistake, then you move on to make another set of mistakes, but again, a small set of mistakes.

Another important consideration is that your checklist items age. This means that if you see that a given item has not caught any defects for a 6 month period, then you need to take it off your list. You have successfully learned new practices and you have effectively eliminated a certain class of defects. This happened to me in the early nineties. Through the use simple techniques, I have eliminated memory leaks from my code.

Q: I just keep adding defects to my list and the list keep growing and growing! Help!

A: Well, this will not be the case. As you work, you will also learn new things and you'll learn to prevent classes of defects. So, if after a while, say 3 to 6 months the "net doesn't catch anything" that is the checklist item fails to detect any defect of that class then you can safely remove that item from your checklist. This means that you have successfully implemented a process improvement step and you have learned to prevent this class of defects.

The only caution is that if you don't find a particular defect because you have changed the domain in which you work and your checklist item was highly domain specific, then you should keep the item on your "domain specific list" and save it for the time when you get back to this domain again.

Q: How fast can you review code in a personal review?

A: Remember, that looking for a defect is almost like sightseeing in a city. Going down the freeway at 60 mph can hardly be considered sight-seeing. However, walking down the sidewalk, you'll be seeing a lot of interesting architecture on the buildings that you are passing by. Similarly, when you review, you can expect that your overall speed is going to be about 200 to 400 lines of code per hour (LOC/hr). This is the equivalent of about 6 to 10 printed pages of code per hour. Of course, this is dependent on the length of your checklist, which in turn depends on your knowledge of domain, environment, tools, etc.

Q: How many defects do you find in a review?

A: The effectiveness of a review is measured by its yield. Going at a rate of 200 to 400 LOC/hr you should expect to get a 70 to 90% yield. This means that if on entry to the review the work product that you are about to review had 10 defects, then on exit from the review you should have found 7 to 9 of those defects. Therefore you still have a few left that you may be able to find by other means, like testing.

Reviews in the TSP

TSP teams are made up developers practicing the PSP. Therefore these teams have a rich set of data to base their decisions on. In addition to personal reviews, these teams also perform peer code reviews; they pick critical code sections to review based on their risk analysis and individual quality data.

The peer code reviews in the TSP follow the capture/recapture method used by estimating animal populations in the wild. This allows the teams to also estimate the number of defects remaining in the product.

The capture-recapture method was originally used to estimate the population of animals in the wild. Here, we are using it to estimate the total number of defects in a set of sources. Assume that T is the total number of defects that need to be found. The first reviewer captures A number of defects. The second reviewer also reviews the exact same set of sources that the first reviewer got. The second reviewer finds B number of defects out of which C number of defects were also found by the first reviewer. Assuming that the second reviewer finds the same proportion of defects in both populations, that is both in the total defect population, and in the population of defects found by the first reviewer, we can write: $A/T = C/B$. Therefore: $T = A * B / C$.

Here is how the capture/recapture method works. Assume:

- A is the number of defects found by the first reviewer
- B is the number of defects found by the second reviewer
- C is the number of defects found by both the first and second reviewer

Based on A, B, and C we can calculate:

- T is the estimated total number of the defects in the product: $T = A * B / C$
- D is the total defect found so far: $D = A + B - C$

- R is the number of remaining defects: $R = T - D$
  $R = (A * B / C) - (A + B - C)$
- Y is the review yield: $Y = D/T * 100$
  $Y = (A + B - C) * C / (A * B) * 100$

If after the review you conclude that the product still has too many defects, then you task two more peers to review the code.

Reviews in CMMI

In the CMMI process model there is a Level 3 process area called Verification. Under this heading the CMMI contains the recommended review goals. The CMMI defines the purpose of Verification as follows "to ensure that the selected work product meets its specified requirements."

The Verification process area has three specific goals:

1. Prepare for Verification
2. Perform Peer Reviews
3. Verify Selected Work Products

In the CMMI reviews are generally considered group activities. There is a recommended process for selecting work products for review. This process is usually risk-based, since the organization uses data to assess the risk of specific activities.

The reviews – as recommended by the CMMI – require preparation, and the results are recorded, which are then fed back into the process for further improvement of the process.

Personal Benefits of Reviews

Reviews allow you to look back at the work you did and force you to clarify and crystallize your thinking. Add to the mix the personal data collection and you get a picture of your intellectual work that arms you for success.

At first your review data may be out of alignment with your self image. After a while though, as you become more comfortable with the data from your personal reviews, you'll implement many small and large personal process improvements, and your performance will invariably improve over time. Be patient: remember that even Tiger Woods needed two and half years to improve his swing between his two victories at the Masters. And the second time he left the pack behind by 15 strokes! You will leave the pack behind, too!

Conclusion

The SEI process models advocate the use of reviews as a means to improve software products, and they also advocate the use of the review data to improve the process that creates those products. Engineers participating in the improvement activities also personally benefit and continually improve their skills and knowledge.

Code Collaborator

Screen-by-screen walk-through for the most popular peer code review tool on the market.

"Although many new software design techniques have emerged in the past 15 years, there have been few changes to the procedures for reviewing the designs produced using these techniques." This observation was made in 1985[1]. Have we learned nothing since Michael Fagan's seminal 1976 paper? Don't changes in development techniques, languages, personnel, and remote sites require us to revisit review practices? Haven't we developed any technology in the past 30 years that might remove drudgery and waste while preserving the proven benefits of code review?

---

[1] Parnas, D. L. and Weiss, D. M. 1985. Active design reviews: principles and practices. *In Proceedings of the 8th international Conference on Software Engineering* (London, England, August 28 - 30, 1985). International Conference on Software Engineering. IEEE Computer Society Press, Los Alamitos, CA, 132-136.

Code Collaborator™ enables peer review by enforcing work-flows, integrating with incumbent development tools, and automating audit trails, metrics, and reporting. It is the culmination of many years of contributions from hundreds of software organizations, all of whom use the tool to improve their code review process.

Code Collaborator replaces traditional formal inspections and over-the-shoulder or email-pass-around reviews with a system that enforces inspection rules, handles diverse workflows, automates audit trails and metrics-gathering, generates reports, and saves developers time through 3rd-party tool integration. Users who are at their keyboards simultaneously can review code with a chat-like interface; users separated by many time zones interact with a newsgroup-like interface. Code Collaborator integrates with SCM systems, issue-tracking, and custom scripts through tools plug-ins and a public Web Services integration API. Reviewers can verify that fixes are properly made by developers before allowing code to be checked into version control.

Solving common peer review problems

There are five specific problems with typical peer code review that Code Collaborator addresses[2].

1. Developers waste time packaging and delivering source code for inspection.

No matter what type of code review you wish to implement, developers will bear the burden of packaging files for delivery. For example, say a developer is preparing for a review of changes that he has not yet checked into version control. After determining which files were added, removed, and modified, he needs to copy them somewhere for transport. He'll also need to extract the

---

[2] Other forms of peer code review have most if not all of these problems. Please see our essay on the types of code review for a detailed treatment of the pros and cons of many classes of review and inspection.

previous versions of those files from version control; otherwise the reviewers will not know what they're supposed to be looking at. (Imagine a change to five lines in the middle of a 2000-line file!) These previous versions must be organized such that reviewers can easily see which current file goes with which previous and can easily run some sort of file-difference program to assist their viewing. And it's easy for the developer to accidentally miss a file he changed.

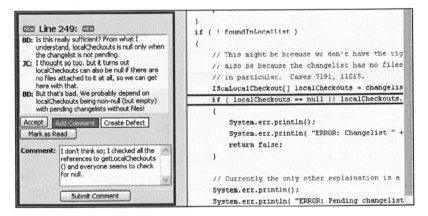

Figure 31: Code Collaborator screenshot showing threaded comments next to Java code under inspection. The author is defending a design decision.

With Code Collaborator, client-side version control integration removes this burden completely. With a single mouse-click or a command-line utility, developers can upload sets of files for review. This can be changes not yet checked into version control as in our example above, or this can be any sets of already-checked-in changes such as differences between branches, labels, dates, or atomic check-in ID's[3].

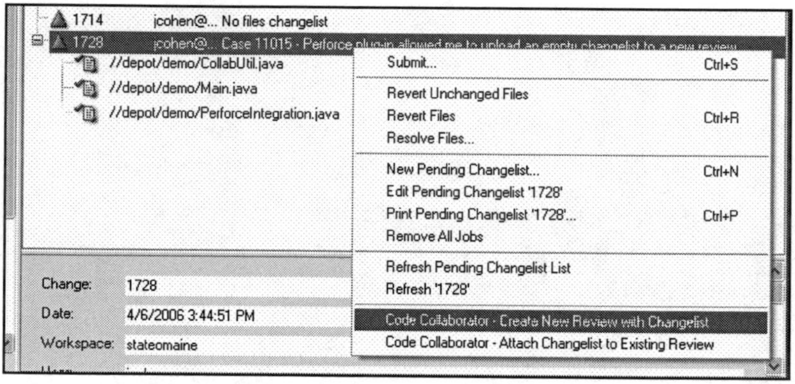

Figure 32: Integration with version control lets Code Collaborator package and deliver source code for review with a single mouse-click. Pictured here is integration with the Perforce® visual client P4V.

Besides saving time on the developer's side, Code Collaborator also removes the burden on reviewers by displaying file differences and allowing reviewers to efficiently comment on individual lines of code without having to write down file names and line numbers.

---

[3] Not all version control systems have the concept of an atomic check-in ID. This is a single identifier that represents a set of files checked in at one time by a single author. In Perforce® this is called a "changelist;" in Source Integrity® it is a "change package," and in Subversion this is a "revision" number associated with a tree snapshot.

2. Don't know if reviews are really happening.

Are developers really reviewing code? Are they perfunctory? With traditional review processes it's impossible to know whether all source code changes have been reviewed.

Code Collaborator provides two mechanisms for enforcing the review process. Review coverage reports allow teams to see how much they've reviewed; with that information they can either fill in the gap or make an informed decision to not review those portions. Or, through server-side version control triggers, Code Collaborator can strictly enforce rules like "All changes made to this branch must be reviewed."

JC	BD	File Relative to: //depot/demo/	Line Number	# of Lines Added (+) Changed (*) Removed (-)		
		CollabUtil.java	[Overall]	+0	*2	-0
	✓		247			
💬	🐞		249			
		Main.java	[Overall]	+14	*0	-12
		PerforceIntegration.java	[Overall]	+8	*0	-0

Figure 33: The file summary list makes it easy for reviewers to see which files were changed, examine prior conversations, and mark defects "fixed" only when verified. New defects can be opened if necessary.

3. Reviewers not verifying that developers are actually fixing defects.

It's one thing send an e-mail saying that something needs to be fixed. It's another to verify that those defects have actually been fixed and that no new defects have been opened in the process. Typical code review processes leave this step to the author, but if no one knows whether reviewers are verifying fixes, the value of pointing out those defects is greatly diminished.

Code Collaborator maintains a defect log for each review, making it easy for an author to see what needs fixing and easy for a reviewer to verify once the author re-submits the fixes. Comments and defects are kept threaded like a newsgroup so it's easy for all parties to refer back to previous conversations.

4. No metrics for process measurement or feedback for improvement.

Developers hate coming up with metrics. No one wants to do a code review holding a stopwatch and wielding line-counting tools. And our field experience is that developers often make up numbers because they forget to start (or stop!) the stopwatch and they tend to invent numbers that they believe make them look good.

Only an automated process can give you repeatable metrics. Code Collaborator collects metrics quietly and automatically so developers aren't burdened. Data include kLOC/hour, defects/hour, and defects/kLOC.

5. Review process doesn't work with remote and/or time-delayed reviews.

Most review processes cannot handle one of the participants being twelve time zones away or even away from the keyboard for a few hours.

Formal inspections, over-the-shoulder reviews, and other in-person reviews don't work unless everyone is in the same place.

E-mail reviews can send data around, but the plethora of conversations and separate reviews can quickly bury a reviewer in e-mail.

Code Collaborator keeps conversations and defects threaded and attached to individual lines of code so it's easy to juggle multiple reviews. It acts like instant messaging when all participants are at the keyboard simultaneously but also like message boards for time-delayed communication.

Anatomy of a review

Most customers follow the standard review workflow described here; system administrators can change this to fit more exactly a desired review process.

Phase 1: Planning

The review begins in the "Planning" phase where the author uploads files for the review and invites the other participants.

Files are either not yet checked in to version control (i.e. review before check-in) or files that have already been checked in (to review after check-in or to review a set of branch changes). SCM integration plug-ins provided by Smart Bear make this typically a one-click or one-command process.

However, any set of files can be uploaded, whether under version control or not. Design and requirements documents can be uploaded, as can arbitrary file-differences generated by comparing directories or from other development tools. For example, you can review the set of changes on a certain branch, or all changes between two dates or labels, or all changes since the last branch integration, just by generating those differences using your version control system and piping them into the Code Collaborator command-line.

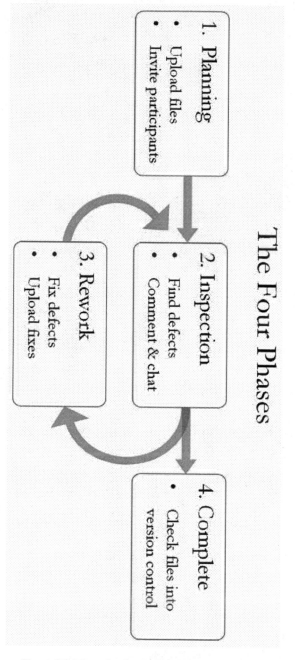

Figure 34: Lifecycle of a review.

There may be other participants, including one or more reviewers and zero or more observers. The former are responsible for careful review, and subsequent review activity will depend on their consensus; observers are invited and can participate but their consensus is never required.

The "Planning" phase is complete when the author decides the correct people are invited and all necessary files are uploaded. The review then enters the "Inspection" phase.

Phase 2: Inspection

When the review switches to "Inspection," e-mails are sent to all participants to alert them the review is starting. For those running the Windows GUI, the taskbar icon will change to indicate that a review is now in progress.

Reviewers are presented with the uploaded files with a side-by-side before/after highlighted difference view (if the files were under version control).

Several options are available for the difference view including: ignore white-space, skip unchanged lines, and whether or not to word-wrap long lines of code. Many common source code files are displayed with syntax-coloring just like an IDE.

Anyone can begin a conversation by clicking on a line of code and typing[4]. Any number of conversations can be going on at once; the associated line of code and an overall review summary view keep the conversation threads distinct and manageable.

---

[4] An important attribute of any developer tool is conservation of movement. It was an important design consideration that starting or responding to a conversation must be as simple as: 1. Click the line of code or conversation, 2. Begin typing. No clicking around or tabbing between GUI elements. If operations are not fast and easy (and optionally keyboard-centric), developers will not use them as much.

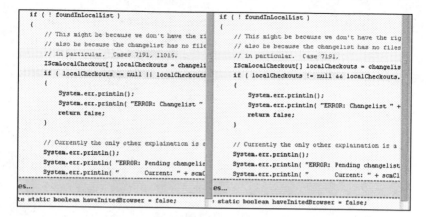

Figure 35: The side-by-side view displays the
same file before and after the proposed changes.

Differences are highlighted. Sub-line modifications are highlighted specially. Source code
syntax is color-coded like an IDE.

Choose between word-wrapped or ganged-
scrollbar views. Options include ignore changes
in white-space and skip unchanged lines.

Comments work a bit like instant message chat and a bit like
newsgroups. If everyone is at the keyboard simultaneously, you
have a real-time "instant message" environment so the review can
progress swiftly. If one or more participants are separated by
many time zones or just aren't currently at the computer, the chat
looks like a newsgroup where you post comments and receive e-
mails when someone responds.

All this implies that Code Collaborator works equally well no
matter where your developers or reviewers are located. In fact,
both methods work at the same time inside a single review! This

means everyone can participate in the manner in which he is most comfortable, and the system will adapt accordingly.

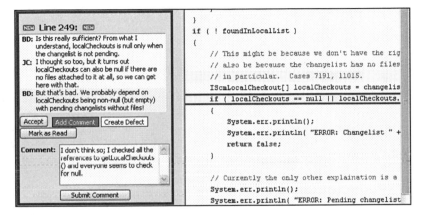

Figure 36: Conversations are threaded by each line of code. To start or join a conversation, just click a line of code and start typing.

The highlighted chat text indicates that the viewer hasn't read that comment yet. By responding or clicking "Mark as Read" he can clear the highlight.

Reviewers open a "defect" for every change the developer will need to make before the review can be deemed complete[5]. Like comments, defects are associated with files and lines of code and show up in the conversations (although you can also create a defect for the review as a whole).

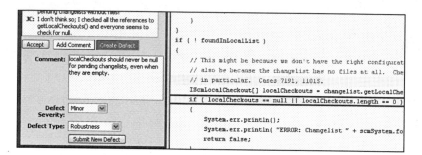

Figure 37: Opening a defect is similar to conversations and is also associated with individual lines of code.

Defects are logged and summarized for the entire review and are also available as part of the metrics and reporting system.

---

[5] Some people object to the word "defect." Some review philosophies insist that words that carry negative connotations should not be used during review. However this is the word used most commonly in the literature and was understood readily by our test subjects in the field.

Are these defects the same as issues from an external issue-tracker used by QA and front-line support? Should Code Collaborator defects be mirrored into the external issue-tracker? Although it is possible to map the two systems, almost none of our customers do. Typically an issue logged into the external system is verified by QA and/or front-level support, however Code Collaborator defects by definition never made it out of development. Often it's not clear what exactly a QA associate would do with a defect. For example, how would he test a defect like "This method needs better documentation" or even something like a null-pointer exception? The exception here is with defects identified in code review but for which you've decided the fix should be deferred. In this case, you need to be able to transform the Collaborator defect into an external issue so you can track it along with other known issues. Collaborator has a facility for this specific use-case.

The "Inspection" phase is complete when all reviewers say it's complete. If defects were opened, the review proceeds to the "Rework" phase; otherwise the review moves to the "Complete" phase.

Phase 3: Rework

In the "Rework" phase the author is responsible for fixing the defects found in the "Inspection" phase.

This might be as simple as fixing a typo in a comment, or as complex as a complete rework of the task involving different files than in the original review.

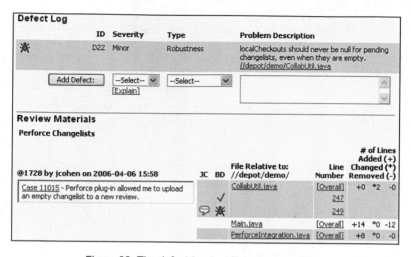

Figure 38: The defect-log and file-summary views
guide the developer during the "Rework" phase
and reviewers during the subsequent follow-up
verification inspection phase.

When the author believes all defects are fixed, she uploads the fixed files to the server and thereby causes the review to re-enter the "Inspection" phase so reviewers can verify the fixes and ensure no new defects have been opened in the process.

If the author (or any other participant) needs to ask a question or otherwise re-open the review, she can do that prior to uploading fixes. The review will also re-enter the "Inspection" phase.

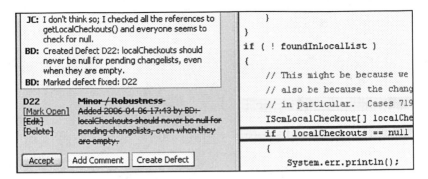

Figure 39: Reviewers examine fixes using the same side-by-side view as the original code inspection.

If the fix is acceptable, the reviewer marks the defect "fixed" by clicking the link next to the defect log located under the conversation history. Displayed here is a defect that was just marked "fixed."

The review is not complete until all defects are marked "fixed" in this manner. New defects can be opened if necessary.

This "round two" of the "Inspection" phase is similar to the first in that conversations can continue, new conversations can start, new defects can be opened, and so on. But this time the reviewers are verifying fixes rather than inspecting fresh code[6].

To "verify," reviewers examine the new changes. If the fix is complete, the reviewer clicks a link next to the defect listing to

---

[6] It is possible for reviewers to cause the review to enter "Rework" before all files have been inspected. This is typical when defects are found that indicate many files will have to be changed, especially with architectural reworks. In this case, "round two" might include much more new-code inspection. Code Collaborator supports this workflow automatically.

indicate that the defect is "fixed." Reviewers can also edit or even delete defects if necessary[7].

This cycle of inspect-rework-inspect is finished when all defects are marked fixed and all reviewers indicate they are finished with the review. At this point the review is officially complete.

Phase 4: Complete

When the review is complete, that's it!

If the author had uploaded some version control changes that weren't yet checked in, the author is sent an e-mail reminding her that the changes may now be committed.

Metrics: Collection, and what to do with it

Developers hate collecting metrics, and they're not good at it. Code Collaborator collects metrics automatically and invisibly, giving product managers the data they need for process improvement.

The three most important metrics collected are: inspection rate, defect rate, and defect density.

The first two are "rates." That is, they answer the question "How long does it take us to do this?" For kLOC[8]/man-hour, often called the "inspection rate," how much code are we able to review per hour of work? For defects/man-hour, often called the "defect rate," how many defects do we find when we spend an hour looking at source code?

---

[7] When should a defect be deleted instead of marked fixed? Deleted means there was never a defect at all – the reviewer was at fault for marking it so. Fixed means there was a problem, but now it's fixed. The distinction is important for metrics, reports, and general communication during the review.

[8] The use of kLOC (thousand lines of code) has been standard practice with metrics analysis for thirty years. It typically refers to physical lines in a file (regardless of white-space, comments, etc.), but some groups ignore white-space and still others ignore comments as well. Typically in code review you need to include comments because you are reviewing comments as well as code.

The third – defects/kLOC – is often called "defect density" in the literature. This indicates the quantity of defects found in a given amount of code.

The most natural question is: What are "good" values for these metrics? And the follow-up: If our metrics are "bad," what can we do to correct the problem? The answers to these questions are complicated. This subject is taken up in several other chapters in this book. See specifically the two chapters on case studies (metrics in the real world), the chapter on metrics and measurement, and the chapter on questions for a review process.

Moving parts

Code Collaborator follows the normal client/server pattern of enterprise software. See Figure 40.

The Server

As with most enterprise-class software systems, a server process acts as the hub, manager, and controller of information. The server has a web-based user interface where users and administrators can do everything – create and perform reviews, configure personal and system-wide settings and run reports.

The server uses an external database to store all data and configuration. This database can be shared across multiple instances of the server for load-balancing or real-time fail-over.

Besides the web-based user interface, the server also hosts a Web Services server. This server is integrated into the same web server as the web-based user interface, so no additional configuration is necessary. You can use Web Services to integrate Code Collaborator into any external systems (SCM server triggers, issue-tracking systems, reporting scripts, intranet portals, data-mining tools, etc.).

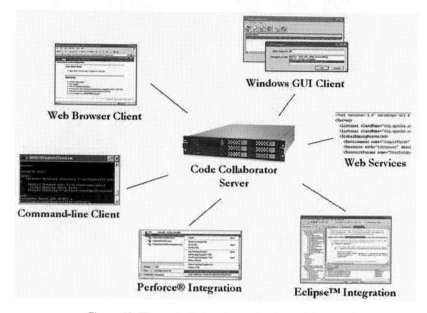

Figure 40: The parts that make up the Code Collaborator system. A server provides central services; many options are available for accessing and manipulating the server data or integrating with 3rd-party tools.

Other Code Collaborator software (such as the command-line and GUI clients) also uses this Web Services interface. We even supply Java- and .NET-based libraries that provide an object-oriented interface to this system.

Command-line Client

Developers will typically install the cross-platform command-line client. This tool lets you upload local files (and file-changes) into new and existing reviews.

Report-generators will also install the command-line client. Although all information in the system can be retrieved through

Web Services, we also support a rich set of reports in a variety of data formats (HTML, XML, CSV) with appropriate filtering options. You can access these reports through the command-line (as well as through the web-based user interface).

Windows GUI Client

Windows users have the option of installing a graphical client to complement the web-based user interface already provided by the server.

The Windows GUI Client provides all the functionality of the command-line client, but in a graphical interface. The client also supports a larger range of version control systems than does the command-line client.

In addition, the Windows GUI Client gives you a taskbar icon that updates to show you whether you have any pending tasks in Code Collaborator.

Perforce® Integration

Perforce users will probably want to install the Perforce Client Integration tools. These are included in the command-line installer.

Integration with P4V and P4Win lets developers upload changelists into new or existing reviews just by right-clicking on the changelist. This works on both "pending" and "submitted" changelists.

We also supply a special tool for use as a Perforce server trigger. For example, you can use this to enforce a rule like "Every commit on this branch requires a review." You can also use this to automatically upload all submitted changelists into Code Collaborator so that you can review code *after* it has been checked in. This can be especially useful with off-shore development groups.

Eclipse™ Integration

Eclipse plug-in integration is currently under development and provides both inside-Eclipse integration as well as a general-purpose cross-platform GUI client that doesn't depend on Eclipse.

Web Services API

The Code Collaborator server publishes a Web Services API based on the widely-used XML-RPC standard. It is easy to communicate with the server on any platform and language.

The command-line, Eclipse plug-in, and Windows GUI clients themselves use this Web Services API. In fact, we additionally wrap the API inside a type-safe, object-oriented, efficient data model and we provide libraries and full documentation in both Java and .NET so you can take advantage of the same technology for your integrations.

There are many reasons why you might want to integrate Code Collaborator with other systems. An issue-tracker integration point might let you synchronize Code Collaborator "defects" with issue-tracker "issues," or you might want to mirror review data (metrics/comments/file-differences) into the associated ticket. A reporting integration point might let you mirror Code Collaborator metrics into your existing reporting system (examples: defects/kLOC, defects/man-hour, kLOC/man-hour, number of defects found of different types or severities).

The Java API is documented on our website: http://demos.codecollab.com/docs/apidocs. The Java implementation libraries are included with the command-line client, and the Code Collaborator User's Manual describes which ones you need and what each of them does, as well as supplying extensive example code showing how to use it.

The XML-RPC API is also documented on our website: http://demos.codecollab.com/docs/apidocs/com/smartbear/ccol lab/datamodel/xmlrpc/IXmlRpcApi.html.

About the Contributors

> *"Who are these people?"*
> *—Jerry Seinfeld*

Jason Cohen

Jason founded Smart Bear Software in 2003 and has ten years of experience in software startups, both VC-funded (GlobeSet, Sheer Genius Software) and bootstrapped (Photodex, ITWatchdogs, Smart Bear). Jason holds a BA in computer science from the University of Texas at Austin.

He lives in Austin with his talented, intelligent, beautiful wife Darla, without whom Smart Bear and this book would not have been possible.

Jason can be reached at jcohen@smartbearsoftware.com.

Steven Teleki

Steven Teleki is a software development manager & mentor. He is Software Development Director at Webify Solutions, Inc. Steve has over 18 years of experience in the software industry; worked on software released to over 40 million customers worldwide; has 3 software patents. He is passionate about solving problems with great software on a schedule and budget that makes the project successful. He focuses on understanding, measuring, and improving individual, team, and organizational software development performance. Steve is Program Chair, also Past Chairman, of the IEEE Computer Society, Austin Chapter. He can be reached at http://steven.teleki.net.

Eric Brown

Eric Brown grew up in Seattle, playing soccer and studying computer science at the University of Washington. He then plunged headfirst into OS/2 development at IBM Boca Raton. After five years at IBM, followed by almost 10 years of writing printer and video drivers on his own, he found the best little software company in Texas, and now spends his days writing code and providing soft drinks for Smart Bear Software.

Eric lives with his wife, Laurie, and children, Rudy and Cait, and sundry pets, in Austin.

Brandon DuRette

Brandon DuRette is the lead software developer for Smart Bear's Code Collaborator product. Brandon's professional experience covers ten years of software development in organizations large and small: everything from IBM to brand new startups. Brandon holds an B.S. in Computer Science from the Massachusetts Institute of Technology where he learned to efficiently transform $C_8H_{10}N_4O_2$ into software.

Brandon resides in Austin with his wife, Crystal, and German shorthaired pointer, Sport.

Steven Brown

Steven Brown is a developer and head of technical support at Smart Bear Software. He was a Distinguished University Fellow at the University of California, Irvine, where he earned an M.S. in mathematical logic and set theory. His B.A. is in computer science from the University of California, Berkeley. In 2003 he won the

USA high score competition for the video game Rayman 3: Hoodlum Havoc.

Steve lives in Austin with his wife Jess and their pets Chewy, Lemma, and The Lynxster.

Brandon Fuller

Brandon Fuller is a Software Engineering Manager with Cisco Systems, Inc. For the past 7 years, he has been responsible for MeetingPlace, an enterprise conferencing solution. He graduated with a Bachelors degree in Computer Engineering from Purdue University. He can be reached at http://brandon.fuller.name/.

Smart Bear Software

Smart Bear Software has been providing tools and mentoring for lightweight code review processes since 2003. Their flagship product, Code Collaborator™, enables peer review by enforcing workflow, integrating with incumbent development tools, and automating audit trails, metrics, and reporting. Smart Bear also creates source code analysis and reporting tools and developer productivity tools.

Smart Bear is the industry thought leader on lightweight code review process and is well known for conducting the largest-ever case study of peer code review at Cisco Systems.

Smart Bear is privately-held and has accepted no venture capital. It is profitable, debt-free, and self-sustaining.

Smart Bear's first product, Code Historian™, was a programmer's utility for visualizing and exploring historical changes in one or more files. We discovered that customers were using the tool mostly for peer code review, and our reaction to feature requests soon lead to Code Reviewer™, the first commercial peer review product. Other customers were more interested in the historical analysis angle that we were uniquely providing and this led to our Code Metrics™ and Code Reports™ products. Still others used Code Pickle™ to implement efficient user sandboxes through "micro-branches" that puts no load or administration on the version control server.

Over the next three years we became the leaders in peer code inspection technology through our unique position in the development tools market and our willingness to sit down with customers to determine how we could genuinely improve their lives.

And the saga continues! Give us a call and see how we can help.

http://www.smartbearsoftware.com
877.501.5651